TAKING THE HIGH ROAD
to Reading, Writing, and Listening

Book 6

By Arlene Capriola and Rigmor Swensen

Phoenix Learning Resources

ACKNOWLEDGMENTS

We deeply appreciate the help so willingly given by many people. In particular, we wish to express our debt and gratitude to Josephine Imwalle for her professional assessment and helpful suggestions; to Francesca Montague for her tireless efforts during all phases of this edition; and to the many students who gave their cheerful and honest feedback.

Text

Every possible effort has been made to trace the ownership of each selection included within this book. If any errors or omissions have occurred, corrections will be made in subsequent printings, provided the publisher is notified of their existence.
Page 2: "The Young Man and the Sea" by Walter Roessing from *Boy's Life*, August 1997. Copyright © 1997 by Walter Roessing. Reprinted by permission of Walter Roessing. Page 6: "I Never Said I Wasn't Difficult" by Sara Holbrook from *I Never Said I Wasn't Difficult*. Copyright © 1996 by Sara Holbrook. Reprinted by permission of Boyds Mills Press. Page 16: "Keeping a Journal: An Interview with Jack Gantos" by Paula W. Graham from *Speaking of Journals*. Copyright © 1999 by Paula W. Graham. Reprinted by permission of Boyds Mills Press. Page 22: "The Cave" by Glenn Dresbach. Copyright © 1996 by Glenn Dresbach. Reprinted by permission of Caxton Press, a division of the Caxton Printers Ltd. Page 26: "The Earth Is Really Moving" by Tony Helies from *Highlights* Magazine, August 2005. Copyright © 2005 by Highlights. Reprinted by permission of Highlights. Page 30: Excerpt from *And to Think that I Saw in on Mulberry Street* by Dr. Seuss, Copyright ™ & copyright © by Dr. Seuss Enterprises, L.P., 1937, renewed 1965. Reprinted by permission of Random House Children's Books, a division of Random House, Inc. Page 37: "The Smell of Money" retold by Sheldon Oberman from *Solomon and the Ant and other Jewish Folktales*. Copyright © 2006 by Sheldon Oberman. Reprinted by permission of Boyds Mills Press. Page 43: "Jumping over Boundaries" by Linda Alvarado from *Highlights* Magazine, November 2005. Copyright © 2005 by Highlights. Reprinted by permission of Highlights. Page 49: "The Harvest That Never Came" by Aaron Shepard from *Cricket*, January 1993. Copyright © 1993 by Aaron Shepard. Reprinted by permission of Aaron Shepard. For more stories and other treats and resources, visit www.aaronshep.com Page 55: "Emme Loves Bees" by Jane Resides from *Highlights* Magazine June 2006. Copyright © 2006 by Highlights. Reprinted by permission of Highlights. Page 62: "In the Days of King Adobe" by Jane Resides excerpted from "In the Days of King Adobe" from *Watch Out for Clever Women*. Copyright © 1994 by Joe Hayes. Reprinted by permission of Cinco Puntos Press, www.cincopuntos.com Page 74: "Frosted Fire" by Sheila Kelly Welch from *A Horse for All Seasons*. Copyright © 2002 by Sheila Kelly Welch. Reprinted by permission of Boyds Mills Press. Page 77: "Speak to Your Class with Confidence" by Ron Kurtus. Copyright © 2005 by Ron Kurtus. Reprinted by permission of Ron Kurtus, Kurtus Technologies, and the School for Champions; www.school-for-champions.com Page 105: "Cooking with the Sun" by Jennifer Davidson from *Highlights* Magazine, January 2006. Copyright © 2006 by Highlights. Reprinted by permission of Highlights. Page 128: "Sea Canary" by Jane Yolen from *If You Ever Meet a Whale*. Copyright © 1990 by Jan Yolen. Reprinted by permission of Curtis Brown Ltd.

Illustrations

Unless otherwise acknowledged, all photographs are the property of Phoenix Learning Resources, LLC.
Cover: stamp: Dr. Seuss © 2004 United States Postal Service. All Rights Reserved. Used with Permission; photos: istockphotos.
Interior: page 2: istockphotos; page 6: istockphotos; page 10: istockphotos; page 11: istockphotos; page 12: istockphotos; page 16: istockphotos; page 17: istockphotos; page 18: Boyds Mills Press; page 22: istockphotos; page 26: istockphotos; page 30: Dr. Seuss © 2004 United States Postal Service. All Rights Reserved. Used with Permission; page 32: istockphotos; page 62: istockphotos; page 63: istockphotos; page 64: istockphotos; page 66: istockphotos; page 67: istockphotos; page 74: istockphotos; page 75: istockphotos; page 77: istockphotos; page 78: istockphotos; page 84: istockphotos; page 85: istockphotos; page 87: istockphotos; page 88: Library of Congress; page 105: Highlights; page 106: istockphotos; page 109: istockphotos; page 128: istockphotos.

Phoenix Learning Resources
910 Church Street • Honesdale, PA 18431
1-800-228-9345 • Fax: 570-253-3227 • www. phoenixlr.com

TABLE OF CONTENTS

■■

SQ3R vi

Unit 1: Reading

Test Taking Skills for Multiple Choice Questions x

A Nonfiction Article: **The Young Man and the Sea** *by Walter Roessing* 1
> Previewing the Lesson: SQ3R
> Objective Questions: Critical Thinking

A Poem: **I Never Said I Wasn't Difficult** *by Sara Holbrook* 5
> Previewing the Lesson: SQ3R
> Objective Questions: Interpreting Poetry

A Social Studies Article: **The Path to Knighthood** 9
> Previewing the Lesson: SQ3R
> Objective Questions: Critical Thinking

An Interview: **Keeping a Journal: Interview with Jack Gantos** *by Paula W. Graham* 15
> Previewing the Lesson: SQ3R
> Objective Questions: Critical Thinking

A Poem: **The Cave** *by Glenn W. Dresbach* 21
> Previewing the Lesson: SQ3R
> Objective Questions: Interpreting Poetry

A Science Article: **The Earth Is Really Moving** *by Tony Helies* 25
> Previewing the Lesson: SQ3R
> Objective Questions: Critical Thinking

A Biography: **It All Depends on How You Look at It** 29
> Previewing the Lesson: SQ3R
> Objective Questions: Critical Thinking

Unit 2: Listening

How to Answer Short Response Questions 36

An Israeli Folktale: **The Smell of Money** *retold by Sheldon Oberman* 37
> Listening Directions: Graphic Organizer
> Short Response Questions: Short Answer Format
> Response Essay: Character Analysis

continued

A Personal Narrative: **Jumping Over Boundaries** *by Linda Alvarado* 43

    Listening Directions: Graphic Organizer

    Short Response Questions: Short Answer Format

    Response Essay: Defending a Position

A Swedish Legend: **The Harvest That Never Came** *by Aaron Shepard* 49

    Listening Directions: Graphic Organizer

    Short Response Questions: Short Answer Format

    Response Essay: Inference

A Science Article: **Emme Loves Bees** *by Jane Resides* 55

    Listening Directions: Graphic Organizer

    Short Response Questions: Short Answer Format

    Response Essay: Point of View

Unit 3: Writing

Tips for Answering Essay Questions 60

Previewing the Lesson: SQ3R 61

A Fiction Story: **In the Days of King Adobe** *by Joe Hayes* 62

    Short Response Questions: Short Answer Format

A Panchatantra Tale: **The Lion and the Hare** *adapted by Lisa Ripperton* 66

    Short Response Questions: Short Answer Format
    Prewriting: Essay Organizer
    Combined Essay: Theme

Previewing the Lesson: SQ3R 73

A Fiction Story: **Frosted Fire** *by Sheila Kelly Welch* 74

    Short Response Questions: Short Answer Format

A Nonfiction Article: **Speak to Your Class with Confidence** *by Ron Kurtus* 77

    Short Response Questions: Short Answer Format
    Prewriting: Essay Organizer
    Combined Essay: Comparison

Previewing the Lesson: SQ3R 83

A Social Studies Article: **King Tutankhamen's Tomb** 84

    Short Response Questions: Short Answer Format

A Social Studies Article: **Secrets of the Underworld** 87

    Short Response Questions: Short Answer Format
    Prewriting: Essay Organizer
    Combined Essay: Drawing Conclusions

Unit 4: Editing Practice
(To be used with Unit 1)

Editing Rules..93
The Young Man and the Sea 96
I Never Said I Wasn't Difficult 97
The Path to Knighthood 98
Keeping a Journal: Interview with Jack Gantos...99
The Cave 100
The Earth Is Really Moving 101
It All Depends on How You Look At It 102

Unit 5: Test
Part I: Reading

A How-To Story: **Cooking with the Sun** *by Jennifer Davidson*.....................105
Objective Questions: Critical Thinking

A Poem: **Four Little Foxe**s *by Lew Sarett* 109
Objective Questions: Critical Thinking

A Hungarian Folktale: **The Outcast** 112
Objective Questions: Critical Thinking

Part II: Listening

A Greek Myth: **The Trojan Horse** 117
Listening Directions: Note taking

Short Response Questions: Short Answer Format

Response Essay: Defending a Position

Part III: Writing

A Science Article: **Whale Watching in Hawaii** 124
Short Response Questions: Short Answer Format

A Poem: **Sea Canary** *by Jane Yolen* 128
Short Response Questions: Short Answer Format
Prewriting: Student's Choice
Combined Essay: Persuasive Argument

Part IV: Editing

Part IV: Editing 133

Editor's Page..134
Guide for **Revising** and **Editing** Essays

About SQ3R  ★ ★ ★ ★ ★ ★ ★ ★ ★ ★ ★ ★ ★ ★ ★ ★ ★ ★ ★

SQ3R is the key to comprehension. The more you know about something before you read it, the better you'll understand it. SQ3R is simple, quick, and efficient.

Study the five steps below.

> *You will use SQ3R for every reading selection in this book.*

SURVEY

Look through the article quickly.
Read the introductory paragraph.
Then look at all:

> headings and subheadings
> captions
> pictures
> italic or boldface print

QUESTION

Read the author's questions at the end of the selection.
They give clues to the reading content as well.

HINT: *Look for the answers when you read the article!*

READ

Read the selections slowly. If what you read does not make sense, it means that you might have read something wrong, REREAD.

> HINT: Sometimes it may be necessary to read something two or more times to understand it.

RECITE

Say what you have read aloud. If you cannot retell it in your own words, it means that you did not understand it. REREAD. It helps to take notes of the facts you have read.

> HINT: Just the act of writing will help you remember the material!

REVIEW

Several days before a test, review your notes. Try to state the information in your own words. Have someone else ask you questions from your notes. In this book at the beginning of each unit, review the techniques for being a smart reader, writer, and test taker.

Unit 1
Reading

Test Taking Skills for Multiple Choice Questions

■ ■

*Be a smart test taker.
Just follow these
suggestions!*

1. Read **all** answers given. Answer "a" may seem like a good answer at first, but answer "d" may be even better.

2. If you think you know an answer, skim through the choices to find it. Then check all the other choices to be sure.

3. Look back at the story for clues to the answer. It helps to underline the proof for your answer.

4. If you are not sure of an answer, circle the question and skip it for now. When you come to the end, go back. Words in other questions may help you remember.

5. NEVER LEAVE A BLANK. It will **always** be marked wrong. Take an "educated guess."

6. An educated guess means that first you cross off all answers you know are wrong. You can usually do this with 2 of the 4 answers. Then you have a 50-50 chance of getting it right. Take a guess.

7. Key words in the questions, such as BEST, MOST, MAINLY are often written in capitals or bold face. Pay special attention to these important words.

8. The words AFTER and BEFORE tell us that the question deals with the sequence of events. Pay special attention to the order of what happened in the story.

9. Be careful of words such as BUT, NOT, and EXCEPT. They signal a change in the question.

10. The wrong answer choices often have words used in the story. Do not be fooled. Look for the right IDEA.

The Young Man and the Sea

SURVEY

After surveying this article, I can tell that:

1. This story is a factual account of a _____.
    a. trip around the world   **b.** boy who fished by the sea

QUESTION

After looking at the questions at the end of the story, I can tell that:

2. The "young man" in the title is _____.
    a. Brian Caldwell   **b.** Walter Roessing

3. Some of the events in this story were _____.
    a. made-up   **b.** life threatening

READ

ANSWER BOX

1. This story is a factual account of a trip around the world.
2. The "young man" in the title is Brian Caldwell.
3. Some of the events in this story were life threatening.

Read the article that follows carefully. If what you read does not make sense, reread!

1

The Young Man and the Sea

by Walter Roessing

Brian Caldwell lay in his sailboat cabin, reading. It was a clear, warm night in the Indian Ocean.

Caldwell, then 19, was trying to become the youngest person to sail solo around the world. He had left his home port of Honolulu, Hawaii, on June 1, 1995. Now it was August 16, and he was en route to the island of Mauritius in the Indian Ocean.

"That's when I heard a deafening roar," Caldwell says. "Before I could move, a huge wave came out of the darkness. It hit with such force that the boat rolled upside-down." Within seconds, the 26-foot *Mai Miti Vavau* — which ironically means "waves from a distant storm"— returned upright, thanks to her keel's heavy lead weight. Caldwell quickly checked to see if the boat was in danger of sinking.

Miraculously, all major structures were okay. But the vessel had suffered lots of minor damage. One sail was torn, a solar panel was broken, and the diesel engine wouldn't start. Everything in the cabin was a mess. A peanut butter jar had broken, and its contents were stuck to the ceiling.

Caldwell could clear the clutter and fix small stuff. But he knew big repairs had to wait for two weeks until he limped into Mauritius.

Deadly Dangers

Before he began his trip around the globe, Caldwell had already logged some 30,000 sea miles. He needed every bit of that experience on his solo voyage.

Near Durban, South Africa, for example, a supertanker missed crushing Brian's boat by a mere 100 yards.

"I knew to stay awake along the South African coast because of the heavy shipping traffic," Caldwell says. "Lots of merchant ships don't have anyone standing watch."

His seamanship also helped him survive huge waves and 80-knot winds near Cape Town, South Africa.

Swimming with a Shark

But his closest call came in the middle of the Pacific Ocean. Several times on his trip, Caldwell dived overboard for a swim or to clean the boat's fiberglass bottom. Each time, he tied a rope between himself and the boat.

"Halfway between Panama and Honolulu, I had just jumped into the ocean when I spotted a shark heading for me," Caldwell says. "It was only 15 feet away when I scrambled back on the boat. It must have been hungry – it circled the boat awhile."

Are We at War?

On one pitch-black night off Australia, Brian spotted a ship following him a couple of miles astern. He radioed the vessel but got no response.

Because those waters are known for pirates, he shut off his cabin lights. The trailing ship did the same.

"Now I was really paranoid," Brian says. "I unfurled full sail and changed my course. The next day, the Australian weather forecast notified mariners of a military exercise in my area—and to stay clear. Maybe I'm lucky I didn't get blown out of the water."

There's Plenty to Do at Sea

With adventures like these, Caldwell says, he was never bored. "I was busy sailing, navigating, taking care of the boat, watching the weather, reading, and cooking," he says. "At every port, I made friends."

He ran up huge phone bills each month reassuring his parents back home he was okay. (Mom wanted to be sure he was flossing his teeth.)

Midway through his journey, the fire-engine-red paint on his boat began to peel. By the time he returned to Honolulu on September 28, 1996—one year, three months, and 27 days later—the vessel looked simply ugly.

But she—and Brian Caldwell—had survived the epic voyage.

Brian Caldwell at a Glance
Born: December 17, 1975, Scottsdale, AZ
Lives: Honolulu, Hawaii
Height: 5 feet, 11 inches
Weight: 164 pounds
Highlights: Became the youngest person to sail solo around the world. Brian will now try to set another record– as the youngest to sail nonstop around the world.

Recite   **Five facts you learned about Brian Caldwell's trip.**

Objective Questions

Circle the letter next to the correct answer.

1. This article is MOST like:
   a. a movie script
   b. a realistic fiction
   c. a legend
   d. a biography

2. What was the MAIN purpose of Brian's trip?
   a. to take a dare
   b. to win a prize
   c. to get world recognition
   d. to make financial gain

3. According to this article, the reason Brian survived the huge wave was:
   a. because of his boat's weight
   b. because of his navigating skills
   c. because the sails were undamaged
   d. because of his ability to repair the boat

4. Which struggle represents the MAIN conflict in this story?
   a. man against age
   b. man against time
   c. man against nature
   d. man against distance

Continue...

5. Read the following sentence from the story.

> **But he knew big repairs had to wait for two weeks until he limped into Mauritius.**

As used in this story, the word "limped" means about the same as:
a. walked lamely
b. sagged to one side
c. sneaked
d. moved with difficulty

6. The information in this article suggests that:
a. Brian's parents were concerned about his well-being.
b. A sailor's club had paid for Brian's trip.
c. Brian's sailboat had non-repairable damages.
d. The Australian government honored Brian for his bravery.

7. All of the following describe difficulties Brian experienced EXCEPT:
a. roving pirates
b. rough seas
c. dangerous fish
d. mechanical breakdown

8. Which sentence from the article represents an opinion?
a. Caldwell could clear the clutter and fix small stuff.
b. Caldwell quickly checked to see if the boat was in danger of sinking.
c. "It must have been hungry–it circled the boat awhile."
d. "At every port, I made friends."

9. Read the following from the story:

> **Several times on his trip, Caldwell dived overboard for a swim or to clean the boat's fiberglass bottom. Each time, he tied a rope between himself and the boat.**

This passage suggests that Brian was:
a. curious
b. cautious
c. adventurous
d. lazy

10. As a result of his experiences, Brian realized:
a. that land is the safest place
b. that caution is more important than speed
c. that he can do even better next time
d. that he is lucky to be alive

For **Editing Practice**, please turn to page 96.

A Poem

I Never Said I Wasn't Difficult

SURVEY

After surveying this poem, I can tell that:

1. In this poem, the speaker _____.
       a. talks about herself   **b.** tells about another person

QUESTION

After looking at the questions at the end of the poem, I can tell that:

2. We know that the speaker is troubled because she talks of _____.
       a. stealing a car   **b.** running away

3. The speaker _____ when someone questions her.
       a. dislikes it   **b.** is thrilled

READ

Read the following poem at least two times. What is the poet's problem?

I Never Said I Wasn't Difficult

by Sara Holbrook

I never said I wasn't difficult,
I mostly want my way.
Sometimes I talk back or pout
and don't have much to say.

I've been known to yell, "So what,"
when I'm stepping out of bounds.
I want you there for me and yet,
I don't want you around.

I wish I had more privacy
and never had to be alone.
I want to run away.
I'm scared to leave my home.

I'm too tired to be responsible.
I wish that I were boss.
I want to blaze new trails.
I'm terrified that I'll get lost.

I wish an answer came
every time I asked you, "Why?"
I wish you weren't a know-it-all.
Why do you question when I'm bored?
I won't be cross-examined.
I hate to be ignored.

I know,
I shuffle messages like cards,
some to show and some to hide.
But, if you think I'm hard to live with
you should try me on inside.

Recite   Recite the problem this poem presents.

Circle the letter next to the correct answer.

1. What is the poet's purpose in writing this poem?
- **a.** to explain
- **b.** to complain
- **c.** to influence
- **d.** to demand

2. Read the following lines from the poem.
> **I've been known to yell, "So what,"**
> **when I'm stepping out of bounds.**

In this poem, the phrase "stepping out of bounds" means:
- **a.** going outside
- **b.** disappearing
- **c.** doing something wrong
- **d.** getting off the court

3. The message of this poem is that the speaker is:
- **a.** annoyed
- **b.** angry
- **c.** content
- **d.** confused

4. The reader can conclude that the poem is about:
- **a.** a six-year old
- **b.** a teenager
- **c.** a young mother
- **d.** a senior citizen

5. Read the following line from this poem.
> **I'm too tired to be responsible.**
> **I wish that I were boss.**

Which conflict do these lines represent?
- **a.** She wants to be guided; she wants to do things her way.
- **b.** Her way is best; others try to stop her.
- **c.** People make her angry; they don't understand.
- **d.** She wants to obey; she wants others to help her.

Continue...

6. The speaker doesn't "run away" because:
   a. she has nowhere to go
   b. she loves her home
   c. she would be punished
   d. she's afraid to

7. In which of the following lines does the speaker tell of her dislike for someone else's questions?
   a. Sometimes I talk back or pout.
   b. I don't want you around.
   c. I won't be cross-examined.
   d. I hate to be ignored.

8. Read the following two lines from the poem.
   I want to blaze new trails.
   I'm terrified that I'll get lost.

   When the poet speaks of blazing new trails, she means:
   a. finding her way home
   b. setting a log aflame
   c. being adventurous
   d. following the path

9. The words, "I shuffle messages like cards" is an example of:
   a. a simile
   b. a metaphor
   c. personification
   d. exaggeration

10. The last line of the poem states, "you should try me on inside." This is the speaker's way of saying:
    a. Try to understand me.
    b. I really love you.
    c. I'm not such a bad person.
    d. It's hard to live with myself.

For **Editing Practice,** please go to page 97.

A Social Studies Article

The Path to Knighthood

SURVEY

After surveying this article, I can tell that:

1. A knight begins his training as a _____.
   a. squire   **b.** page

QUESTION

After looking at the questions at the end of the story, I can tell that:

2. Reading and writing were skills taught by the _____.
   a. knight   **b.** priest

3. One job of a page was to _____.
   a. wait on the lady of the castle   **b.** go off to battle for the squire

READ

ANSWER BOX

1. A knight begins his training as a page.
2. Reading and writing were skills taught by the priest.
3. One job of a page was to wait on the lady of the castle.

Read the article that follows carefully. If what you read does not make sense, reread!

The Path To Knighthood

Step 1:
Becoming A Page

During the Middle Ages, the sons of noble families were raised to be knights. Training started early. A boy of seven would no longer live at home with his family, but would be sent to the castle of another lord. First he would be a page, learning courtesy and obedience by waiting on a lady. He would also wait at the table, serving the knights. At this stage of his education, the page might learn to play an instrument. If the priest of the castle had time, he would teach the page to read and write.

The page spent a lot of time preparing to be a champion in battle. He learned about armor by helping his lord dress for jousts and battles. Many days were spent playing on wooden horses, practicing with small wooden swords and shields. The young page began to work with falcons and hawks, hunting birds, to perfect his skills as a hunter.

Step 2:
Life As A Squire

By the time the boy became 14 years old, he was made a squire and became a knight's apprentice.

Now things took a more serious turn. The squire still served at the table, but now he learned to carve the meat. A squire practiced sword

> apprentice = trainee or pupil

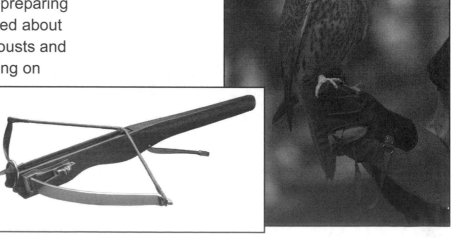

fighting against a wooden stake, and then with other squires. Now he trained his horse to be unafraid of battle noises. He also rode with one arm free to hold the lance.

Practicing for the jousts, or battle games, was a dangerous event. A large, heavy sack was hung from a post and was the target. Just as the squire approached the sack, he would stand up in the stirrups and thrust the lance with all his might. If he hit the target smack in the middle, he was safe. If he was off, the sack swung around from the blow, and hit him in the back of the head.

> stirrups = footholds on the side of the saddle

As he grew older, a squire followed his knight into battle to help if he fell. At this time, the squire was getting used to the weight of the heavy armor he would soon be wearing. When the knight who trained him thought he was ready, usually between 18 and 21 years of age, the squire would be dubbed a knight.

Step 3:
A Knight Is Dubbed

The night before the ceremony, the squire who was to be dubbed a knight spent the night in a vigil, that is, he prayed in the chapel all night, watching over his armor. At sunrise he took a symbolic bath, to show he was clean in body and soul.

> symbolic = something that stands for an idea

In the morning, he dressed in clothes that had symbolic colors. Red was for his blood, white for purity, and brown because he would return to the earth when he died.

When he presented himself to the knight, a sword was placed around his waist. Then golden spurs were tied to his ankles. When the knight took a sword and tapped him on the shoulder, the squire officially became a knight.

After the ceremony, the knight prepared a great feast for the squire who would take his place. There was a tournament where the new knight joined the joust for the first time.

Recite the three steps to knighthood.

Circle the letter next to the correct answer.

1. Children who became pages usually came from:
   a. the lower classes of society
   b. the nearby city
   c. important families
   d. orphanages

2. Read these lines from the story:

   If the priest of the castle had time, he would teach the page to read and write.

   This information shows that:
   a. the priest sometimes helped the teacher
   b. reading and writing were unimportant skills for knights
   c. only squires learned to read
   d. there were no books

3. The author most likely wrote this article to:
   a. entertain the reader
   b. record recent events
   c. correct a mistaken idea
   d. inform the reader

4. What was the MOST important reason for the page to wait on a lady in the castle?
   a. He was too young for any other job.
   b. She had many children to care for.
   c. The lord was not home to help her.
   d. He learned manners by doing so.

5. After reading the article, the reader can conclude that the lord might have several knights in training at one time. This is because:
   a. Squires needed to practice with others.
   b. Many servants were needed.
   c. Squires were often killed in jousts.
   d. Castles were large, lonely places.

Continue...

6. Which task below was a symbolic part of the squire's preparation?
   a. the training of birds
   b. the dress for the ceremony
   c. practicing for the jousts
   d. serving the meat

7. Why was it important to work with falcons?
   a. Meat had to be hunted.
   b. Falcons made good companions.
   c. It was the hobby of knights.
   d. Falcons represented the gods.

8. A joust at the feast of a new knight did NOT give him a chance to:
   a. appear before a crowd
   b. show his skills in jousting
   c. have fun at this party
   d. kill the enemy

9. From the article you can conclude that the knight had 3 qualifications.
   He had to be:
   a. a gentleman, a religious man, a warrior
   b. a musician, a falconer, a fighter
   c. clean, educated, handsome
   d. wealthy, brave, carefree

10. The flow chart below shows the 3 steps to Knighthood.

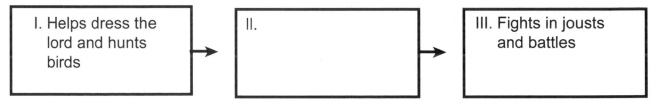

| I. Helps dress the lord and hunts birds | → | II. | → | III. Fights in jousts and battles |

Which event BEST fits in the second box?
   a. dresses in symbolic colors
   b. lives with his own family
   c. plays war games and trains his horse
   d. has many squires

For **Editing Practice,** please go to page 98.

An Interview

Keeping a Journal: Interview with Jack Gantos

SURVEY

After surveying this article, I can tell that:

1. Jack Gantos is a writer of _____.
   a. fiction   **b.** biographies

QUESTION

After looking at the questions at the end of the story, I can tell that:

2. Mr. Gantos began his journal _____.
   a. when he was a young child   **b.** when he was in his teens

3. The author confesses to _____.
   a. copying from his sister's journal   **b.** stealing his brother's journal

READ

ANSWER BOX

1. Jack Gantos is a writer of fiction.
2. Mr. Gantos began his journal when he was a young child.
3. The author confesses to copying from his sister's journal.

Read the next article carefully. If what you read does not make sense, reread!

Keeping a Journal:
Interview with Author Jack Gantos
by Paula W. Graham

I envied my sister's journal.

It was my sister's idea. She was two and a half years older, an adult as far as I was concerned. Compared to her I was pond scum. I was also a huge copycat. Anything my older sister did, I had to do, too. She got a journal, one of those year diaries with a lock and key. I thought I would lose my mind because I figured it was about the coolest thing I'd ever seen. And, I thought the key was awesome. Part of the key thing was because my mother wouldn't let me lock the bathroom door because she thought I might go in and fill up the tub and drown myself. When I saw my sister's journal with the key, the reason I wanted a journal was because I wanted the key, and the reason I wanted the key was because I thought I could lock the bathroom door. I made life very unpleasant for my mother until I got the journal and then, of course, the key didn't fit the bathroom lock.

Second-Grade Rat

I got my first journal in the second grade and it was a significant piece of private property, of great importance to me, just as important as a button is to Corduroy.

When I was getting early advice from my sister, I remember saying to her one day, "Well, what should I write about?" And she said, "Simple, write about what you love," and that was very good advice. I loved food. I was a huge eater as a child so I kept a menu of everything I ate. I'd have the journal with me, so if I chewed gum, I'd write down "chewed gum," and I'd save the wrapper and tape it in. Some of those early journals have more stuff in them than writing.

I'll tell you how I kept my sister from snooping in my journal. I was riding my bike down the street one day and I saw a road-kill mouse. I scraped it up and put it in the front of my journal. So I had a scab-like flattened mouse on the title page. That protected my journal. Of course, I was snooping in hers because I found out those little keys fit every journal on the planet. I would go into her bedroom, open her drawer, take it out, unlock it, and copy entire passages from my sister's journal into mine. It was the moment I realized I could write better than my sister.

Adolescence

Adolescence was a time of friendships. One thing that was predominant in those diaries was the social life—people you knew, people you wanted to know, secret crushes. I had absolutely no spine. I was really a gutless kid. When it came to being around girls, I couldn't even talk to girls. Everything would make it into the journal.

A Writer's Journal

Keeping a journal is the first thing I talk to kids about. I show them my journals, show them several. I tell them this is the single most important book that they will write. Whether they become poets or novelists, or better business letter writers, that's fine. I hope they do. At the end of their lives, the books they are going to be most satisfied with are their journals. It's a good writing habit, and it's a way to discover important truths about yourself.

No Lost Journals

I don't have any lost stories. Of my two hundred volumes, I've never lost any. It would set me back years. I always put my address and phone number on the inside of my journal and I put down Reward Offered. I'm thinking of taping a $20 bill on the inside with a note: "Here's twenty bucks, this is just the beginning of the reward." You lose these things and it's like your house burning down.

Jack Gantos's books include:

Heads or Tails: Stories from the Sixth Grade
Jack's New Power: Stories from a Caribbean Year
Jack's Black Book
Joey Pigza Swallowed the Key
Desire Lines
The Rotten Ralph Series of Picture Books

Jack Gantos in the Sixth Grade

Recite three benefits to keeping a journal.

Circle the letter next to the correct answer.

1. The MAIN idea in this interview is:
    a. Journal writing is fun.
    b. Journal writing is a way to learn about yourself.
    c. Journal writing is most important for young children.
    d. Journal writing is a path to a successful career.

2. According to this interview, Jack's sister helped him in all the following ways EXCEPT:
    a. He got the idea of a journal from her.
    b. She told him what to write about.
    c. He learned he was a good writer from her journal.
    d. She lent him her journal.

3. Why did the writer MOST LIKELY include facts about the "road kill?"
    a. to show how much he wanted to keep his journal private
    b. to prove he was an average 7-year old
    c. to amuse and entertain the reader
    d. to explain the subject matter of his earliest journals

4. Which of the following statements from the journal expresses an opinion?
    a. It was my sister's idea.
    b. Some of those early journals have more stuff in them than writing.
    c. I tell them this is the single most important book that they will write.
    d. Of my two hundred volumes, I've never lost any.

5. Why was Mr. Gantos MOST fascinated wth a journal at such a young age?
    a. His older sister had one.
    b. He wanted privacy in the bathroom.
    c. He liked to get his own way.
    d. He loved the idea of his own key.

Continue...

6. Jack compares his journal to Corduroy's button in order to show:
   a. how much he values it
   b. that it is a childish thing
   c. he was a big eater
   d. that it is a private thing

7. According to Mr. Gantos, how is a journal MOST useful to teenagers?
   a. It is a way to develop good writing habits.
   b. It is often the first book they write.
   c. It helps them write what they cannot always say.
   d. It is a way for them to share with their friends.

8. The author MOST LIKELY copied lines from his sister's journal:
   a. to prove he was the better writer
   b. because he liked to steal her secrets
   c. as proof that he had read her journals
   d. because he was bored with his own journal

9. Read the following sentence from the story.
   Compared to her I was pond scum.

   As used in this article, the term "pond scum" means?
   a. a dirty little kid
   b. a thin and frail child
   c. worthless
   d. a spoiled child

10. Why hasn't the author lost any of his journals?
   a. He has offered rewards to those who find them.
   b. He has written his name and address on the inside cover.
   c. He has kept them together in a large box.
   d. He has treated them with great care.

For **Editing Practice,** please go to page 99.

The Cave

■ ■

S U R V E Y

After surveying this poem, I can tell that:

1. The setting for this poem is probably _____.
    a. an out-of-the-way area   **b.** a popular picnic spot

Q U E S T I O N

After looking at the questions at the end of the poem, I can tell that:

2. The main character in this poem is _____.
    a. an old man   **b.** a boy

3. While at the cave, the main character _____.
    a. saves an owl   **b.** lights a fire

R E A D

ANSWER BOX

1. The setting for this poem is probably an out-of-the-way area.
2. The main character in this poem is a boy.
3. While at the cave, the main character lights a fire.

Read the poem through once. Then read again and stop after each stanza. If what you read does not make sense, reread!

The Cave

by Glenn W. Dresbach

Sometimes when the boy was troubled he would go
    To a little cave of stone above the brook
And build a fire just big enough to glow
    Upon the ledge outside, then sit and look,
Below him was the winding silver trail
    Of water from the upland pasture springs,
And meadows where he heard the calling quail;
    Before him was the sky, and passing wings.

The tang of willow twigs he lighted there,
    Fragrance of meadows breathing slow and deep,
The cave's own musky coolness on the air,
    The scent of sunlight … all were his to keep.
We had such places—cave or tree or hill…
    And we are lucky if we keep them still.

Recite   **Describe the view from the cave.**

Objective Questions

Circle the letter next to the correct answer.

1. What is the MOST important reason for the boy's trip to the cave?
   a. to enjoy the beauty of nature
   b. to work through a problem
   c. to build a fire
   d. to go exploring

2. Where is the cave in this poem?
   a. beside a brook
   b. in a meadow
   c. in the desert
   d. on the flat part of a cliff

3. Read the following line from the poem.
   And we are lucky if we keep them still.

   In the line above, the word "them" refers to:
   a. the wilderness
   b. private place to think things over
   c. a cave or tree or hill
   d. the sky and passing wings

4. Why did the boy light a fire?
   a. to cook a meal
   b. to keep warm
   c. to enjoy its light
   d. to declare his anger

5. Which word BEST describes the tone of this poem?
   a. angry
   b. peaceful
   c. impatient
   d. thoughtless

6. Read the following lines from the poem.
   The cave's own musky coolness on the air,
   The scent of sunlight...all were his to keep.

   When the poet says he could "keep" these things, he means:
   a. keep a secret
   b. take home
   c. remember
   d. protect

Continue...

7. According to this poem, which living creatures share the boy's surroundings?

    a. birds

    b. frogs

    c. snakes

    d. willows

8. The chart below shows ways that the poet uses the senses.

Seeing Upon the ledge outside, then sit and look	Hearing And meadows where he heard the calling quail
Smelling	Tasting The tang of willow twigs he lighted there

Which line from the poem BEST fits the empty box?

    a. We had such places—cave or tree or hill...

    b. Fragrance of meadows breathing slow and deep

    c. And build a fire just big enough to glow

    d. Before him was the sky, and passing wings.

9. This poem is MOST LIKELY written by:

    a. a poet who does not know the boy

    b. a young boy feeling troubled

    c. an old man giving advice to people

    d. a man who was the main character in the poem

10. The main idea of this poem is:

    a. nature and solitude can chase away troubles

    b. sometimes it is good to have a place to hide

    c. a fire is a soothing thing

    d. a cave is a special place

For **Editing Practice,** please go to page 100.

The Earth Is Really Moving

■■■■■■■■■■■■■■■■■■■■■■■■■■■■■■■■

S U R V E Y

After surveying this article, I can tell that:

1. This article was probably written to_____.
   a. create a sense of mystery   **b.** explain a scientific fact

Q U E S T I O N

After looking at the questions at the end of the story, I can tell that:

2. The author compares the earth's movement to _____.
   a. a merry-go-round   **b.** a rolling ball

3. People _____ that the earth travels around the sun.
   a. have always known   **b.** did not always know

R E A D

ANSWER BOX

1. This article was probably written to explain a scientific fact.
2. The author compares the earth's movement to a merry-go-round.
3. People did not always know that the earth travels around the sun.

Read the article that follows carefully. Stop after each section. If what you read does not make sense, reread!

The Earth Is Really Moving

by Tony Helies

Long ago, people believed the Earth didn't move. They saw the Sun rise every morning, travel across the sky, and set every evening. The stars and moon crossed the sky each night. Naturally, people thought that the sun, moon, and stars were moving, not the Earth.

But if the Earth were spinning, the sun, moon, and stars would also appear to move across the sky. Which is right?

Scientists tell us the Earth is moving. It rotates on its axis once every day, and orbits around the sun once each year.

As the Earth spins, it rotates at 1,000 miles per hour at the equator. And the Earth and all the people on it are orbiting at 67,000 miles per hour to make the trip around the sun in 365 days.

So why doesn't it feel like we are spinning like a top and rocketing through space? The reason is that we can't always feel motion, even if we are traveling very fast.

When we are riding in a car at 60 miles per hour on a smooth straight road, can we feel the motion? We feel it only when the car is speeding up, slowing down, turning, or bouncing up and down on a bumpy road. We don't feel motion when we are going at a constant speed in a straight line.

On a merry-go-round, we feel motion because we are not traveling in a straight line. A spinning Earth turns like a merry-go-round. So why can't we feel it? The answer is that although our speed is high, we change direction very slowly. We wouldn't feel the merry-go-round moving if it took a full day to make one turn. Our orbit around the sun also takes a long time — a whole year — so we don't feel that motion either.

Today we know the Earth does move. Experiments can detect the slow change of direction of the Earth's motion. For example, the back-and-forth path of a pendulum swinging at the North Pole would rotate 360 degrees in 24 hours as the Earth turns.

Long ago, people traveled on horseback, in coaches, and on ships — all of which gave a pretty bumpy ride. This made them believe that they could always feel motion. Today we know that we feel changes in motion only when they occur rapidly.

The Earth is definitely moving. We can't feel it because, luckily for us, it's a nice smooth ride.

Recite Recite three facts you learned about our Earth.

Objective Questions

Circle the letter next to the correct answer.

1. The author concludes that we CANNOT feel the Earth moving because:
   a. it travels very slowly
   b. it rotates at the equator
   c. it moves at the speed of light
   d. it makes gradual changes in direction

2. Which word below does the author use to indicate the Earth's movement around the sun?
   a. spinning
   b. rocketing
   c. orbiting
   d. rotating

3. As proof of the Earth's movement, the author points to:
   a. the pendulum
   b. the merry-go-round
   c. the earth's axis
   d. a spinning top

4. When traveling by car, people do NOT feel the motion if the car:
   a. slows down
   b. speeds up
   c. makes a wide U-turn
   d. travels steadily at 80 mph.

5. The MAIN purpose of this article is to:
   a. inform
   b. entertain
   c. alert
   d. amuse

Continue...

6. Read the following sentence from this story.
> **Experiments can detect the slow change of direction of the earth's motion.**

The word "detect" means about the same as:
- **a.** chart
- **b.** discover
- **c.** label
- **d.** measure

7. For many years, people were convinced that the Earth stood still. All of the following led to this belief EXCEPT:
- **a.** the sun's position in the sky
- **b.** the path of the moon
- **c.** the fact that they felt no movement
- **d.** the lack of wind

8. The main conflict in this article is between:
- **a.** common sense and scientific proof
- **b.** seeing and believing
- **c.** speed and direction
- **d.** movement and lack of movement

9. From the facts in this article, the reader can conclude that the Earth's rotation is slowest:
- **a.** in the morning
- **b.** at night
- **c.** at the equator
- **d.** at the North and South Poles

10. The author compares the Earth's movement to a merry-go-round. He concludes that we feel the movement of the merry-go-around because of its:
- **a.** speed
- **b.** size
- **c.** path
- **d.** location

For **Editing Practice,** please go to page 101.

It All Depends on How You Look at It

After surveying this article, I can tell that:

1. The famous author, Dr. Seuss, is known for his _____.
     a. children's stories   **b.** adult fiction

After looking at the questions at the end of the story, I can tell that:

2. One of the books Dr. Seuss wrote is _____.
     a. *Alice in Wonderland*   **b.** *And to Think That I Saw It
                                          on Mulberry Street*

3. Dr. Seuss was also _____.
     a. a composer   **b.** an illustrator

ANSWER BOX

1. The famous author, Dr. Seuss, is known for his children's stories.
2. One of the Books Dr. Seuss wrote is *And to Think That I Saw It on Mulberry Street*.
3. Dr. Seuss was also an illustrator.

Read the next article that follows carefully. Stop after each section.
If what you read does not make sense, reread!

THEODOR SEUSS GEISEL

USA 37

2004

A Little About Dr. Seuss' Life

When an author is interviewed, people always ask, "Where do you get your ideas?" When a book surprises us with a great story and unusual illustrations, curiosity gets the better of us. We want to know why a book makes us laugh, or makes us sad, or angry.

Sometimes a biography explains where an artist gets ideas. It tells the story of a person's life. That gives us some ideas about how an artist thinks. However, something else must play a part in creating a book or a painting.

Let's take a look at the things that influenced Theodor Seuss Geisel, or Dr. Seuss. He is best known for the famous children's books he wrote and illustrated. However, Seuss also used his talents to teach and entertain adults. He and a friend, Mr. Eastman, created Private Snafu, whose name means "Situation Normal — All Fouled Up." Snafu was featured in training films showing servicemen what not to do. So you can guess that Private Snafu was a funny character. He also drew cartoons for major magazines that were popular during the 1930s and 40s.

Dr. Seuss' First Children's Book

The idea for his first children's book, *And To Think That I Saw It on Mulberry Street,* came to him while he was sailing across the Atlantic Ocean. The rhythm of the ship's engines set a rhyme going in his head.

The words in the poem move like the constant beat of the ship's engines. When you read, words and pictures in the book seem to be in motion.

Seuss imagines a young boy walking home from school. Part of the poem goes like this:

All the long way to school
And all the way back,
I've looked and I've looked
And I've kept careful track.
But all that I've noticed,
Except my own feet,
Was a horse and a wagon
On Mulberry Street.
That's nothing to tell of,

That won't do, of course...
Just a broken-down wagon
That's drawn by a horse.
That *can't* be my story. That's only a *start*.
I'll say that a ZEBRA was pulling that cart!
And that is a story that no one can beat,
When I say that I saw it on Mulberry Street.

His Sources of Inspiration

What a zany story this turns out to be! Where did he get his inspiration for the illustrations of this poem? He must have loved his hometown, Springfield, Massachusetts. That city is the setting of this book and several others. Seuss' father was the curator of Forest Park Zoo in Springfield. Perhaps the zoo animals inspired his wacky animal drawings.

Twenty-eight publishers rejected Dr. Seuss' first children's book. One day Seuss ran into an old friend who was a publisher. He liked the book. *And To Think That I Saw It on Mulberry Street* finally came out in 1937. "See," said Seuss, "everything has to do with luck."

The Cat in the Hat Appears

In 1954, *Life* magazine published an article saying kids were not learning to read. It said that children's books were too boring. Dr Seuss' publisher asked him to write a book using only 250 words. Seuss produced a book using 220 words, and called it *The Cat in the Hat*. It had his quirky drawings, rhyme, and rhythm and an interesting story. And it was easy enough to be read by beginning readers.

Seuss once said, "I like nonsense, it wakes up the brain cells. Fantasy is a necessary ingredient to living. It's a way of looking at life through the wrong end of the telescope."

Whether writing for adults or children, Seuss relied on fantasy for his stories. But his inspiration sprang from the things he saw, the places he'd been, and the people he knew.

Recite   **Recite five facts about Dr. Seuss' life.**

Objective Questions

Circle the letter next to the correct answer.

1. What is the main purpose of this article?
   a. to persuade the reader to write poetry
   b. to correct certain myths about Dr. Seuss
   c. to tell of another side to Dr. Seuss
   d. to show how interviews *should* be conducted

2. Which statement below can you infer from this article?
   a. *The Cat in the Hat* was Dr. Seuss's first successful book.
   b. Dr. Seuss's books for adults won him recognition.
   c. Working with animals led to Dr. Seuss's career choice.
   d. Dr. Seuss had a different way of viewing the world.

3. According to this article, where did Dr. Seuss get the inspiration for many of his drawings?
   a. his experience with the army
   b. the place where he grew up
   c. the ship on which he sailed
   d. a *Life* magazine article

4. Which technique does Dr. Seuss use MOST to make his books fun?
   a. exaggeration
   b. quotations
   c. suspense
   d. surprise endings

5. What did the beat of the ship's engines inspire?
   a. the meaning of the poem
   b. the story of the poem
   c. the length of the poem
   d. the rhyme of the poem

Continue...

6. According to this article, all of the following influenced Dr. Seuss' work **EXCEPT:**
   a. his home
   b. the zoo
   c. reading problems
   d. his teachers

7. The thread that runs through most of Dr. Seuss children's books is:
   a. honesty
   b. fantasy
   c. safety
   d. responsibility

8. Which topic below does the author NOT address in the article?
   a. Dr. Seuss's educational background
   b. Dr. Seuss's real name
   c. Dr. Seuss's childhood
   d. Dr. Seuss's artistic skills

9. The author states that *The Cat in the Hat* "had its quirky drawings."
   The word "quirky" means about the same as:
   a. colorful
   b. false
   c. unusual
   d. accurate

10. Dr. Seuss's MAIN goal in writing *The Cat in the Hat was:*
    a. to show how clever cats can be
    b. to write a good read-aloud book for children
    c. to write a book with rhythm
    d. to limit the number of different words

For **Editing Practice,** please go to page 102.

Unit 2
Listening

How to Answer Short Response Questions

It's easy to answer questions that ask you to explain something.

Follow these steps:

- **Start your first sentence using Part of the Question (P. O. Q.)**
- **Back up what you state with story facts (for example: "In the story...")**

Let's take the story of Goldilocks and the Three Bears

1. Why did the three bears go for a walk in the woods?

Answer: <u>The three bears</u> went <u>for a walk in the woods</u> so that the porridge would have time to cool off. In the story it said that the porridge was too hot to eat.

2. What was the first thing Goldilocks did?

Answer: <u>The first thing Goldilocks did</u> was to taste the porridge. In the story it says that she tasted both Papa and Mama Bear's porridge. Then she ate all of Baby Bear's porridge.

3. What kind of person do you think Goldilocks is?

Answer: <u>I think that Goldilocks is</u> a very curious person. The story says that she wanted to know how the porridge tasted, how the chairs felt, and how the beds were. She got into a lot of trouble because she was so curious.

As you get used to this kind of question, you may want to change the words you use.

Remember:
- to **answer the question that is asked.**
- to back up your answer with **information from the story.**

Listening Comprehension

The Smell of Money

retold by Sheldon Oberman

Listening Directions

You are going to listen to a story called, "The Smell of Money." The story will be read twice. You may take notes on the story anytime during the two readings. You may wish to use the space below or the graphic organizer on the next page.

Remember to refer to your notes to answer the questions that follow.

Notes

Graphic Organizer

■ ■

Setting
(Where and when does it happen?)

Main characters

Problem
(What does the character want or need?)

Events
(What happens in the story?)

-
-
-
-

Solution
(How is the problem solved?)

Short Response Questions

■■■■■■■■■■■■■■■■■■■■■■■■■■■■■■■■■■■■
Use the information from the story to answer the questions below.

1. In the graphic organizer below, explain why the girl smelled the bakery goods and why the baker felt she needed to pay for this.

Why the girl smelled the bakery goods	Why the baker felt she needed to pay

2. Read these lines from the story;

   "Baker," said Solomon. "Do you care so much about money that you want to be paid even for the air around you?"

Explain what King Solomon is really trying to tell the baker.

_____

_____

_____

_____

_____

Short Response Questions

■ ■

3. If asked to choose a different title for this story, what would you choose? Explain why your title would be an appropriate one.

_____

_____

_____

_____

_____

_____

_____

_____

Essay

■ ■

Many legends tell of King Solomon's wisdom. His clever reasoning led to many fair decisions in the court cases he judged. Write an essay showing how "The Smell of Money" is a key example.

In your essay, be sure to include:
- what dispute he was called upon to decide
- how his decision was both clever and fair

Use information from the story to support your answer.

_____

_____

_____

_____

_____

_____

_____

_____

_____

_____

_____

Essay

■ ■

_____

_____

_____

_____

_____

_____

_____

_____

_____

_____

_____

_____

_____

_____

_____

_____

_____

To **Revise** and **Edit** your essay, go to page 134.

Jumping Over Boundaries

by Linda Alvarado

■ ■

Listening Directions

You are going to listen to a story called, "Jumping Over Boundaries." The story will be read twice. You may take notes on the story anytime during the two readings. You may wish to use the space below or the graphic organizer on the next page.

Remember to refer to your notes to answer the questions that follow.

Notes

Graphic Organizer

■■■■■■■■■■■■■■■■■■■■■■■■■■■■■■■■■■■■

Setting

Problem

Main characters

Events

Solution

Short Response Questions

■■■■■■■■■■■■■■■■■■■■■■■■■■■■■■■■■■■

Use the information from the story to answer the questions below.

1. There are many kinds of prejudice. In the chart below describe the role that prejudice played in the life of Linda Alvarado.

Example of prejudice by the school	Example of prejudice by society
How she overcame it	**How she overcame it**

2. How were Mrs. Alvarado's actions an example of bravery?

_____

_____

_____

_____

_____

_____

Short Response Questions

■■■■■■■■■■■■■■■■■■■■■■■■■■■■■■■■■

3. Explain the author's statement, "This wasn't just about me."

_____

_____

_____

_____

_____

_____

_____

_____

_____

Essay

■ ■

The author refers to this quote by Robert Frost:

Two roads diverged in a wood, and I,
I took the one less traveled by.
And that has made all the difference.

Write an essay showing how the lines of this poem describe Linda Alvarado's life.
In your essay be sure to include:
- the "less traveled" path she took in her childhood
- the "less traveled" path she took as an adult
- what difference her choices have made

_____

_____

_____

_____

_____

_____

_____

_____

_____

_____

_____

Essay

■■

_____

_____

_____

_____

_____

_____

_____

_____

_____

_____

_____

_____

_____

_____

_____

_____

_____

_____

_____

_____

To **Revise** and **Edit** your essay, go to page 134.

The Harvest That Never Came

by Aaron Shepard

Listening Directions

You are going to listen to a story called, "The Harvest That Never Came." The story will be read twice. You may take notes on the story anytime during the two readings. You may wish to use the space below or the graphic organizer on the next page.

Remember to refer to your notes to answer the questions that follow.

A word you need to know:

testament = proof

Notes

Graphic Organizer

■ ■

Setting

Main characters

Problem

Events

Solution

Short Response Questions

■ ■

Use the information from the story to answer the following questions below.

1. Complete the graphic organizer to show two ways that Arild's crop was different from most crops. Use details from the story in your answer.

Arild's crop	Most other crops
1. 2.	1. 2.

Short Response Questions

■ ■

2. Through no fault of his own, Arild is faced with overwhelming problems. Explain his problems and the strange facts that caused them.

_____

_____

_____

_____

_____

3. What kind of man was King Erik? Describe his sense of humor and the two ways he was helpful to Arild.

_____

_____

_____

_____

_____

_____

_____

Essay

■ ■

Arild Ugerup proved himself to be both intelligent and resourceful. Write an
essay in which you explain this statement. Show the outcome of Arild's scheme.

In your essay be sure to:
- explain what Arild did to demonstrate his intelligence and resourcefulness
- describe how he benefited from his actions

Use details from the story to support your answer.

_____

_____

_____

_____

_____

_____

_____

_____

_____

_____

_____

_____

_____

Essay

_____

_____

_____

_____

_____

_____

_____

_____

_____

_____

_____

_____

_____

To **Revise** and **Edit** your essay, go to page 134.

Emme Loves Bees

by Jane Resides

Listening Directions

You are going to listen to a story called, "Emme Loves Bees." The story will be read twice. You may take notes on the story anytime during the two readings. You may wish to use the space below or draw an organizer on the next page.

Remember to refer to your notes to answer the questions that follow.

A word you need to know:

smoker = a device that blows smoke to quiet bees in a hive

Notes

Notes

■■

Short Response Questions

Use the information from the story to answer the questions below.

■■■■■■■■■■■■■■■■■■■■■■■■■■■■■■■■■

1. Based on the information in the story, "Emma Loves Bees," fill in two requirements for beekeepers in each column in the chart below.

Items Necessary for Successful Bee Keeping

Clothing Needed	Supplies Needed
1.	1.
2.	2.

2. Explain why it is clever to plug the queen's cage with sugar candy.

_____

_____

_____

3. Give two reasons why it is helpful to have other people in the family also be beekeepers.

_____

_____

_____

_____

Essay

■ ■

Emma believes that beekeeping is an entertaining and fascinating hobby.
Yet this article mentions some negative aspects of beekeeping as well. Write
an essay in which you describe both the pros and the cons of this hobby.
Do you agree that beekeeping is a worthwhile hobby for a child?

In your answer be sure to:
- describe the pros and cons of beekeeping as a hobby
- discuss whether or not you agree that beekeeping is a worthwhile
  hobby for a child

Use details from the story to support your answer.

_____

_____

_____

_____

_____

_____

_____

_____

_____

_____

Essay

∎∎∎∎∎∎∎∎∎∎∎∎∎∎∎∎∎∎∎∎∎∎∎∎∎∎∎∎∎∎∎∎∎

_____

_____

_____

_____

_____

_____

_____

_____

_____

_____

_____

_____

_____

_____

To **Revise** and **Edit** your essay, go to page 134.

Unit 3 Writing

Tips for Answering Essay Questions

1. Read the test question at least two times. Underline the words that tell you what to do. If you are still not sure, ask your teacher.

2. Use a graphic organizer to take notes before writing your essay. Your essay will be more organized.

3. Often the bullets given are keys to the paragraphs. If you write one paragraph for each bullet, you will have answered the question fully. Add a brief introduction and conclusion to your essay.

4. Write as neatly as possible. If your teacher can't read what you have written, you will not get full credit.

5. If your essay requires more lines than you are given, just draw an arrow and continue writing where space permits.

6. When your essay is complete, just stop—even if there are lines left. Students often write more to fill up the spaces given. Their answers go off topic, spoiling their essays.
   (Also applies to Short Response Questions)

7. When you are done, reread both the question and your answer. Did you answer all parts of the question?

8. At the end, go to the **Editor's Page** in this book on page134.

A Fiction Story

In the Days of King Adobe

A Panchatantra Tale

The Lion and the Hare

SURVEY

After surveying these stories, I can tell that:

1. The word, "adobe," used in the first story, also means _____.

    a. a kind of Indian   **b.** a kind of brick

2. The second story will probably deal with _____.

    a. man versus beast   **b.** predator versus prey

QUESTION

After looking at the questions at the end of each story, I can tell that:

3. I will be asked to_____.

    a. decide the lesson both   **b.** write about the
         stories teach   importance of folktales

READ

Read the stories carefully. If what you read does not make sense, reread!

In the Days of King Adobe

by Joe Hayes

■■■■■■■■■■■■■■■■■■■■■■■■■■■■■■■■■■

There was once an old woman who lived all alone in a tiny house at the edge of a village. She was very poor, and all she had to eat was beans, tortillas, and thin cornmeal mush.

But the old woman was very thrifty, and by saving carefully, a penny a day, she was able to buy herself a big ham. She kept it hanging from a hook in a cool, dark closet behind the kitchen.

One evening a couple of young men who were traveling through the country stopped at the old woman's house and asked if they could have lodging for the night. The woman welcomed them. "I'm happy to have the company. I'll get busy and make us all a good supper," she said.

She got out her pots and pans and then went to the closet and cut three slices from the ham–two thick, generous slices for the travelers and a thin one for herself. The young men were delighted to see the old woman preparing ham for their supper. Seldom were they offered such good food in their travels. But those two young men were a couple of rascals, and right away a roguish idea came into their minds. They decided to steal the ham that night while the old woman was asleep.

After they had all eaten their fill, the old woman spread out a bed for the young men on the floor. She said good night and wished them good dreams and then went into her own room to sleep.

When they felt sure the old woman was asleep, the young men got up and crept to the closet. They took the ham down from the hook and wrapped it in a shirt. One of the young men put the ham in his traveling bag. Then the two young men lay down to sleep with smiles on their faces. They had very good dreams indeed!

But the old woman hadn't gone to sleep either. When she heard the young men getting up from their pad on the floor, she went to the door and peeked out. She saw everything the young men did.

Later that night, when the young men were sound asleep, the old woman crept from her room. She took the ham from the traveling bag and hid it under her bed. Then she wrapped an adobe brick in the shirt and put it in the traveling bag.

At breakfast the next morning, one of the young men winked at the other as he sat down at the table and said, "Abuelita, last night I dreamed that today my friend and I would be eating good food all day long."

abuelita = Spanish for grandmother

"Is that right?" the old woman replied. "Tell me more about your dream. I'm fascinated by dreams. I believe they are sometimes true."

The young man smiled at his friend and said, "I dreamed we were sitting under a tree eating. It was a beautiful land. And the king of that country was named Hambone the First."

"Aha!" spoke up the second young man. "Now I remember that I had the same dream. And I remember that the land in which Hambone the First was king was named Travelibag."

"I had a similar dream last night myself!" she exclaimed. "I was in a land named Travelibag, and Hambone the First was king of that country. But then he was thrown out by the good people and replaced by a new king named Adobe the Great. And for some people, that meant a time of great hunger had begun."

The two rascals joked about the old woman as they traveled down the road. At midday, they sat down under a shady tree to rest.

"Well, now," said the first young man as he leaned back and closed his eyes. "Don't you think it's time for dreams to come true? Here we are sitting under a tree, just as I dreamed. Open up the land of Travelibag. My stomach tells me I need to visit the king of that land."

"By all means," said the other. "Let's see how things are going with our old friend, Hambone the First."

The young man opened his bag and pulled out the bundle wrapped in his shirt. Chuckling to himself he slowly unwrapped the shirt. Suddenly the smile disappeared from the young man's face. "Oh no!" he gasped. "The old woman knew more about dreams than we thought."

"What do you mean?" asked the other.

"Well," he said, "she told us Hambone the First had been thrown out, didn't she?"

"Yes."

"And do you remember who was put in his place?"

The young man laughed. "Adobe the Great! Where do you suppose she came up with a name like that?"

"Probably right here," said his friend. "Look."

The first young man opened his eyes. "I see what you mean," he groaned. "And I see what the old woman meant about the time of great hunger beginning. I'm starved!"

After several hungry days, the two men met another kind old woman who fed them a good meal. This time they didn't even think about trying to play any tricks.

Short Response Questions

■■■ ■ ■■ ■ ■■ ■ ■■ ■ ■■ ■ ■■ ■ ■■ ■ ■■ ■ ■■ ■ ■■ ■ ■ ■

Use the information from the story to answer the questions below.

1. Fill in the chart below to show how the young men in the story changed their attitude toward old people from the beginning of the story to the end.

Young men's attitude toward old people at the beginning of the story	Young men's attitude toward old people at the end of the story

2. Circle the word you think BEST describes the old woman in the story, "In the Days of King Adobe."

curious   **clever**   **witty**

Explain the reason for your choice. Use details from the story to support your answer.

_____

_____

_____

_____

_____

_____

The Lion and the Hare

adapted by Lisa Ripperton

■ ■

There was a beautiful meadow, which was the home of many wild animals. They would have lived very happily there had it not been for one mischief-loving Lion. Every day this Lion wandered about, killing many helpless creatures for the mere sport of the slaying. To put an end to this, the animals gathered in a body, and going to the Lion, spoke to him in this way, "King Lion, we are proud to have such a brave and valiant beast to rule over us. But we do not think that it is fitting for one of your rank to hunt for his own food. We therefore wait upon you with this request: Henceforth you remain quietly at home, and we your subjects will bring to your lair such food as it is fitting that a king should eat."

The Lion, who was greatly flattered, immediately accepted their offer.

Thus every day the animals drew lots to decide who among their number should offer himself for the Lion's daily portion. In due time it came about that the lot fell upon the Hare. Now the Hare, when he learned that it was his turn to die, complained bitterly.

"Do you not see that we are still tormented by that Lion?" he asked the other animals. "Only leave it to me, and I will release you for all time from his tyranny. "

The other animals were only too glad at these

> tyranny = cruel and unjust use of power

words, and told the Hare to go his way. The Hare hid for some time in the bushes, and then hurried to the Lion's lair. By this time the Lion was as angry as he was hungry. He was snarling and lashing his yellow tail on the ground. When he saw the Hare, he called out loudly.

"Who are you, and what are my subjects doing? I have had no morsel of food today!"

The Hare besought him to calm his anger and listen to him.

"The lot fell today," he began, "on another hare and myself. In good season we were on our way here to offer ourselves for your dinner, when a lion sprang out of the bushes and seized my companion.

In vain I cried to him that we were destined for the King's table, and, moreover, that no one was permitted to hunt in these royal woods except your Majesty. He paid no heed to my words save to retort, – 'You do not know what you are saying. I am the only king here. That other Lion, to whom you all bow down, is a usurper.' Dumb with fright, I jumped into the nearest bush."

usurper = one who takes over power

The Lion grew more and more indignant as he listened to the Hare's tale.

"If I could once find that lion," he roared, "I would soon teach him who is king of these woods."

"If your Majesty will trust me," answered the Hare, humbly, "I can take you to his hiding place."

So the Hare and the Lion went out together. They crossed the woods and the meadow, and came to an ancient well, which was full of clear, deep water.

"Yonder is the home of your enemy," whispered the Hare, pointing to the well. "If you go near enough, you can see him. But," he added, "perhaps you had better wait until he comes out before you attack him."

These words only made the Lion more indignant. "He shall not live a moment after I have laid eyes upon him," he growled.

So the Hare and the Lion approached stealthily to the well. As they bent over the edge and looked down into the clear water, they saw themselves reflected there. The Lion, thinking that it was the other lion with the other hare, leaped into the well, never to come out again.

Short Response Question

■■■■■■■■■■■■■■■■■■■■■■■■■■■■■■■■■■

Use the information from "The Lion and the Hare" to answer the question below.

3. Read the following line from the story.

>**"Only leave it to me, and I will release you for all time from his tyranny."**

Explain what the hare meant by this statement. What action did he take to back up his promise?

_____

_____

_____

_____

_____

_____

_____

Prewriting

■ ■

AFTER reading the **Essay Questions** on page 71: Fill in the essay organizer below. You may also use the next page for notes. Your notes will help you write your essay.

List information from *both* the story and the tale.

An explanation of the lesson	How characters from "In the Days of King Adobe" proved the lesson	How characters from "The Lion and the Hare" proved the lesson
Your Notes	Your Notes	Your Notes

Prewriting Notes

Essay

■ ■

Both "In the Days of King Adobe" and "The Lion and the Hare" deal with deception. Which lesson below BEST relates to both stories?

- **Deception does not always lead to positive results.**
- **Trickery knows no size or age.**
- **Honesty is the best policy.**

Write an essay in which you explain the lesson that relates to BOTH stories. Describe how the main characters of each story prove the lesson to be correct.

In your answer be sure to include:
- an explanation of the lesson you chose
- a description of how the characters from each story proved the lesson to be correct.

Use details from BOTH stories to support the information in your essay.

_____

_____

_____

_____

_____

_____

_____

_____

_____

_____

GO ON to page 72 if you need more space.

Essay

To **Revise** and **Edit** your essay, please go to page 134.

A Fiction Story

Frosted Fire

A Nonfiction Article

Speak to Your Class with Confidence

■■■■■■■■■■■■■■■■■■■■■■■■■■■■■■■

SURVEY

After surveying the story and the article, I can tell that:

1. Frosted Fire is probably _____.
    a. a horse's name   **b.** a type of fire

2. The second article deals with _____.
    a. overcoming fear   **b.** using confidence to help others

QUESTION

After looking at the questions at the end of the two selections, I can tell that:

3. I will be asked to discuss _____.
    a. ways the two selections are   **b.** how the two selections
        alike and different   affect the reader

READ

ANSWER BOX

1. Frosted Fire is probably a horse's name.
2. This article deals with overcoming fear.
3. I will be asked to discuss ways the two selections are alike and different.

Read the two selections that follow carefully. If what you read does not make sense, reread!

73

Frosted Fire

by Sheila Kelly Welch

Repeatedly her father had told her, "He's not the same horse. He's changed." But Sara had refused to believe him.

"Easy, honey," she whispered to Frosty as she rubbed beneath his dark mane. But she felt no relaxation in the horse's tense body.

Focusing her gaze on the low jump at the far end of the shed, she tried to suppress her misgivings. Carefully, lightly, she pressed her legs against Frosty's sides, urging him into a trot. He sprang forward too fast and became unbalanced, unsteady. She'd been working with him for weeks, going over all the basics, yet he didn't feel ready.

As they cantered toward the low hurdle, it seemed to grow into a solid and forbidding wall. A clutch of fear grasped Sara's throat as she pulled him to a halt.

With her brother Jay trailing behind, she led Frosty back to the stables. Maybe he wouldn't jump anymore, but at least he belonged to her now. Officially. She'd always thought of Frosty as her horse, even though he'd been foaled at her uncle's horse farm. She had been the one to ride him for two unforgettable years, winning in one show after another. When Uncle Matt was offered an incredibly high price for his young champion, he couldn't resist.

Unfortunately for Frosty, he'd been bought by the parents of a young girl with inadequate riding experience. When she'd tried to jump him, she'd fallen off, hanging on to the reins, and given the horse's tender mouth a vicious yank.

Unable to control the now-skittish horse, they contacted Uncle Matt to complain. Sara's parents offered to buy Frosty. He had come home a few weeks before Christmas, thin and frightened, but finally hers.

That night Sara flopped on her rumpled bed, exhausted and discouraged. When a screaming noise woke her, she reached her clock and pushed the button, but the wail went on and on.

A smoke alarm!

Instinctively, she rolled out of bed and hit the floor, groping her way toward the window. In the tarry blackness, she could smell smoke— even taste it.

Outside on the snowy ground, Sara hugged Jay and her mom."We've got to call the fire department!" her father said.

"Hank, no! You can't go back inside." Her mother grabbed hold of his pajama shirt-tail. They all stared silently at the smoke coming from their escape windows in sinister, shimmering puffs.

"I'll call from the Bancrofts," said Sara. "On Frosty, I can cut across the fields."

With a quick nod, Sara urged Frosty from the barn. Across the wide pasture they galloped, plowing through drifts that would have trapped a person on foot.

Somewhere up ahead was the rail fence that separated their property from the Bancrofts'. But where was it?

Then she saw a dark set of lines etched in snow. She jumped off before Frosty had completely stopped. But when she tried to swing the gate open, it wouldn't budge. One side was frozen to the ground, beneath a snowdrift.

A sob caught in her throat, but inside her mind was racing. She remounted and trotted Frosty away, then turned him to face the fence. Suddenly her fear of the jump was gone. Her fear, Frosty's fear— she understood now that it was all mixed.

Sara could feel the horse gathering himself beneath her, and then he plunged into a canter. It was a smooth, high jump, with no hesitation, no mistake. They swept across the field and up Bancrofts' lane.

"Fire! Fire!" Sara screamed, riding right up to the porch steps. After a long, dreadful moment, the porch light flooded on, the door swung wide, and there was Mrs. Bancroft.

She ran down the steps and helped Sara off her horse. "Call the fire department!" she yelled to her husband as he came to the door.

Later, Sara was standing next to her family and the Bancrofts, who had brought her home. "Smoke damage," said Mr. Bancroft. "Bad, but sure could've been a lot worse."

"You can thank Sara," said Mrs. Bancroft, "and her horse. Isn't that the same horse she rode in all those shows?"

Sara looked at her father. In the pale light that was beginning to seep across the eastern sky, she saw him nod as he said, "Yes, he's the same horse."

Short Response Questions

Use the information from the story to answer the questions below.

1. Complete the chart below to describe the main problem Sara faced and how she solved it.

Sara's main problem	How she solved the problem

2. What realization helps Sara overcome her difficulty with her horse?

_____

_____

_____

_____

_____

_____

_____

Speak to Your Class with Confidence
by Ron Kurtus

Have you ever had to speak in front your class—perhaps to give a report—and you got real nervous? Perhaps you stammered, started to sweat, and even started to shake. Many students have this problem. In fact, the fear of speaking in front of a group is one of the worst fears people have. It even ranks above the fear of death (but not as great as the fear of snakes).

Some questions you may have about this subject are:
- Why am I so afraid?
- What can I do about it?

This article will answer those questions and explain some ideas about how you can speak to your class with confidence.

What are you afraid of?

One big reason students get so nervous when they have to speak in front of their class is because they have a fear of looking stupid in front of their fellow students. This fear holds for all people, when they have to speak in front of others.

Another major fear is that you will forget what you were going to say or that your mind will go blank, such that you will just stand there like an idiot, while everyone watches you. You fear that you will look so stupid in front of the whole class that they may laugh and make fun of you. What a terrible feeling!

Tips to overcome those fears:

There are several tips or tricks to use to overcome the fear of making a mistake or looking foolish when you speak to a group:

Know your subject matter:

If you are going to speak to the class about something, you should know the subject matter thoroughly. Since it is usually something you have just been studying, you should be able to answer questions from students who aren't as familiar with the subject as you. You should always know more than the material you are presenting, so you can answer questions. Knowing the subject matter gives you a feeling of confidence before you give your talk.

Know your speech:

A big fear students have is that they will forget what they were going to say, especially if they must speak without notes. You should know your speech or talk very well before presening it in front of a class or an audience. Don't try to wing it. Rather, write it out ahead of time and practice it.

Reduce fear of your audience:

Speaking to important people or dignitaries can create fear in a person. This fear can be overcome by visualizing the people as not all that important. One trick is to imagine that the audience is all in clown outfits. This ridiculous image will make them seem not all that important. It is surprising how such an image can relax you.

Remember that they are just other kids and that they are there to hear what you have to say.

Practice, practice, practice:

Practice is extremely important. The more you give a talk, the more automatic it

becomes, the more meat it can have, and the more confidence you have in your abilities to give the speech. Practice alone, to small groups, and to friends. Practice.

Feel confident:

The more you successfully do something, the more confidence you have that you can do it again—even better.

Not only do you want to be able to get through your ordeal of talking in front of your class, you want to be able to feel confident before you do it and like a champion when you are through.

Short Response Question

■ ■

3. Explain how confidence plays a key role in a person's performance. Use details from the article to support your answer.

_____

_____

_____

_____

_____

_____

Prewriting

■ ■

AFTER reading the **Essay Question** on page 81: Fill in the essay organizer below.
You may also use the next page for notes. Your notes will help you write your essay.

List information from *both* the fiction story and the nonfiction article.

Similarities between the two fears	Differences between the two fears	Steps a person may take to conquer each fear
Your Notes	Your Notes	Your Notes

Prewriting Notes

Essay

■ ■

Both the story and the article you read deal with fear. Although the fears are different, they are similar in many ways. Write an essay in which you compare the two fears discussed. Discuss the actions a person might take to conquer each fear.

In your answer, be sure to:
- describe the similarities and differences between the two fears discussed
- discuss steps to take to conquer each fear

Include information from both the story and the article to support your answer.

_____

_____

_____

_____

_____

_____

_____

_____

_____

_____

_____

_____

GO ON to page 82 if you need more space.

Essay

To **Revise** and **Edit** your essay, please go to page 134.

Tutankhamen's Tomb
Secrets of the Underworld

S U R V E Y

After surveying these two articles, I can tell that:

1. In the first article, the tomb discovered was that of a _____.
    a. king   **b.** slave

2. The second article deals with _____.
    a. archeology   **b.** Greek mythology

Q U E S T I O N

After looking at the questions at the end of the articles, I can tell that:

3. I will be asked to evaluate _____.
    a. the quality of someone's work   **b.** changes over time

R E A D

ANSWER BOX

1. In the first article, the tomb discovered was that of a king.
2. The second article deals with archeology.
3. I will be asked to evaluate changes over time.

Read the following articles carefully. If what you read does not make sense, reread!

King Tutankhamen's Tomb

The Valley of the Dead in Egypt has fascinated people for centuries. It is the burial ground of many pharaohs, the ancient kings of Egypt. The pharaohs had unlimited power. They ran the government and the army. They also had enormous wealth.

The tombs of the pharaohs lie buried under the Egyptian desert sands. These tombs are large. Some have several rooms. The ancient Egyptians believed in life after death.

They developed a process that preserved bodies for centuries. After the body was placed in a cask, the face of the dead person was painted on the top. They also filled the tombs with all kinds of treasure. The pharaoh would be just as rich in the next world as he had been in this one.

For thousands of years, robbers have searched for the tombs. Sometimes raiders have found them. They would steal a hoard of wealth.

During the early 1900s, another type of treasure hunter became interested in the Valley of the Dead. Archeologists arrived on the scene. They believed they could learn about the culture of ancient Egypt from the tombs.

King Tutankhamen Uncovered

Lord Carnarvon from England had the money to finance a "dig" in the Valley of the Dead. Carnarvon and the archeologist Howard Carter unearthed the tomb of the boy pharaoh, Tutankhamen, in 1922. It lay protected under the dry desert sands.

Although Tutankhamen was only 18 years old when he died, his tomb revealed a life of magnificent splendor. It took time and money to uncover these remains of a past civilization.

After many years of expensive digging and searching, Carter dug up a stairway. It led to a long hall ending in a door bearing the name Tutankhamen. Behind the door lay a wealth of treasure. There were life-size statues standing guard. A golden throne had a panel behind it showing the king and queen. They had faces of red glass and headpieces of turquoise. In the next room, workers found ivory chairs, and alabaster vases. But there was no sign of a cask or a mummy.

Finally, Carter came to the room containing Tutankhamen's mummy. It was in a gold cask covered with semi-precious stones. His face and arms were painted on it in detail.

The final room, the Treasury, contained the riches for Tutankhamen's new life. There were weapons, games, baskets, sandals, pottery, and many other things. There was evidence that some of the buried gold and silver had been stolen long ago.

The Curse?

A king, who lived 33 centuries ago, revealed the life and customs of his times. However, with the discovery, came the Curse of Tutankhamen. Anyone disturbing the tomb would pay. Shortly after the tomb was discovered, Lord Carnarvon died. Did he die from a mosquito bite as claimed, or from the curse?

Short Response Questions

■ ■

Use the information from the story to answer the questions below.

1. Explain how archeologists knew that they had uncovered the remains of a very important person.

_____

_____

_____

_____

2. Describe Lord Carnarvon's fate after the discovery. What do you believe was the cause?

_____

_____

_____

_____

_____

_____

_____

Secrets of the Underworld

■ ■

Archeologists study people. They investigate old things and sites. Archeologists are a hardy bunch. They dig everywhere. They even poke into garbage piles and toilets. They want to know everything about ancient people. How did they make tools? Why did they move around? What kinds of food did they eat?

Underwater Archeologists

A little water won't stop archeologists. These scientists work underwater. They use the same methods as archeologists on land. They dig up rock shelters. Divers explore abandoned ships and airplanes. Their work tells us about seafaring life and culture. What kind of cargo did this ship carry? Did it sink during wartime?

The water surrounding Florida is a graveyard for thousands of ships. Perhaps they were the victims of shifting sands. Perhaps they caught on coral reefs. Some must have gone down in fierce hurricanes. Today, these shipwrecks are time capsules. They tell the history of sea trade. They give a lot of background on colonies in America. What countries did explorers come from? What goods were they bringing with them? When did they come? Who came after them? Who won the new land? The changing fortunes of European powers show up in these wrecks.

Historical Archeologists

Do you like to read diaries, letters, and maps? Then historical archeology might be for you. These historians gather information from documents and records. Then they compare it with what they find at sites.

We found out many things we didn't know from the James Robinson House. It is an African American homestead. The house was built before the Civil War. Today visitors can see the building in Manassas National Park in Virginia.

Robinson was born in 1799, a free African American. When he had earned $484, he bought 170 acres of land. Soon he built a small log cabin on the land in Manassas, Virginia. As years went by, the family turned it into a prosperous farm. James Robinson became one of the wealthiest African Americans in the Manassas area.

Unfortunately, the house stood in the middle of what later became a Civil War battlefield. It was almost destroyed in 1861 and 1862. The North and the South fought two bloody battles near his home. After the war, the Robinson family restored the house.

In 1993, the Robinson House burned down.   While it was being rebuilt, archeologists found important documents. These papers showed that Robinson and an enslaved woman named Susan Gaskin had six children. The children were born into slavery. Susan and four of the children were the property of John Lee. Discovered contracts proved that James Robinson bought some of his children out of slavery. Some charred bricks revealed that Robinson had not been able to free all his children. But those children had found a way home. They had carved their names on the fireplace bricks.

Robinson House in the 1840s

Archeologists are busy all over the world. They are digging and hoping. They are digging underground and under the water. Their discoveries provide us with new and exciting historical insights.

Short Response Question

■ ■

3. Archeologists just discovered a Spanish ship, dating from the 1600s in the Florida "graveyard." They found a compass, a cargo of guns, gold, and wine. What does this tell you about people traveling to America at that time?

_____

_____

_____

_____

_____

_____

Prewriting

AFTER reading the **Essay Question** on page 91: Fill in the essay organizer below.
You may also use the next page for notes.

List information from **both** articles.

	what the discoveries revealed about the past	how our culture has changed since they lived
King Tutankhamen		
James Robinson		

Prewriting Notes

■ ■

Essay

■■■■■■■■■■■■■■■■■■■■■■■■■■■■■■■■■■■■■■■

Archeologists study and preserve parts of our past. This knowledge helps us evaluate the changes that have taken place. What insights into history do King Tutankhamen's tomb and the James Robinson papers give us about the past?

In your essay be sure to include:
- what these two discoveries have taught us about the past
- how our culture has changed since each of these men lived

Include information from BOTH selections to support your answer.

_____

_____

_____

_____

_____

_____

_____

_____

GO ON to page 92 if you need more space.

Essay

■ ■

_____

_____

_____

_____

_____

_____

_____

_____

_____

_____

_____

_____

_____

_____

_____

_____

_____

_____

To **Revise** and **Edit** your essay, please go to page 134.

Editing Rules

■ ■

To edit your paper you must check for mistakes in punctuation, capitalization, and usage. Here are some rules to help you.

Capitalization:

1. Names of cities:
Chicago, Detroit, Miami, Austin, San Francisco

2. Names of states:
Texas, Maine, Colorado, Mississippi, Florida

3. Names of countries and nationalities:
France, the French people; China, the Chinese people

4. Names of streets and roads:
Ross Street BUT We drove down the street

5. Days of the week:
Monday, Tuesday, Wednesday, etc.

6. Months of the year:
January, February, March, April, May, etc.

7. Titles when they go before a name:
Mr., Mrs., President Lincoln, First Lady Martha Washington
BUT I saw the president on TV.

8. Major words in titles of books, movies, and songs.
Articles (a, an, the), prepositions (at, in, on), and conjunctions (and, but, if) are not major words and are **NOT** capitalized in titles.
A Tree Grows in Brooklyn, Ice Age

9. General words when they are used as names:
Is Mother at work?
Did Father say he would be home by 6:00 pm?
BUT I've seen your mother at all of our games.

10. The first word in a quote:
John said, "Let's go swimming."

End Punctuation:

1. A period ends a sentence. One idea is finished.

2. A question mark ends a question. Are you ready?

3. An exclamation point says WOW!

Commas:

1. In a list of three or more:
Remember to bring sandals, suntan lotion, and a swimsuit.

2. In a date, separate day and year:
May 15, 2010

3. In an address, separate city and state:
We live in Northfield, Minnesota.

4. In the greeting and closing of a friendly letter:
Dear Jennifer,
Your friend,

5. Just before a quote:
Joe said, "Meet me in the park."

Apostrophes:

1. To show possession:
The girl's umbrella   Charles' friend

2. In contractions:
do not becomes don't
it is becomes it's   Example: Eat pizza while **it's** still hot.
BUT no apostrophe when "its" shows possession
Example: The dog lost its collar.

Usage means how we put words together:

1. Check words that sound the same, but have different meanings:
I go <u>to</u> the store. I like apples, <u>too</u>. <u>Two</u> of us have new toys.

2. Check subject-verb agreement:
Be sure all the kids <u>is</u> in the car.   FIX Be sure all the kids <u>are</u> in the car.

3. Check tense agreement:
Last week I <u>go</u> on vacation. FIX Last week I <u>went</u> on vacation.

In a final check be sure:
• that every sentence has a subject and a predicate which states what
 that subject is doing.

• that you have avoided any sentence fragments – they do not express
 complete thoughts.

• that you also avoided run-on sentences made of two complete sentences
 run together without punctuation to separate them.

Editing Practice

Practice your editing skills below after completing the lesson on pages 1 – 4.

The Young Man and the Sea

■■■■■■■■■■■■■■■■■■■■■■■■■■■■■■■■■■

Here are two paragraphs a student wrote about orienteering. There are mistakes in each paragraph. Some sentences may have one or more mistakes. Other sentences may contain no mistakes at all. <u>There are no mistakes in spelling.</u>

Read the paragraphs to find the mistakes. Draw a line through each mistake in the paragraph. Then write the correction above it.

Orienteering has recently become a popular sport. People ask, "do I need to buy special equipment for this sport." For orienteering you need good shoes, a map, and a compass. A course is set in the wilderness. You must use your skills. To find your way through a series of checkpoints.

Orienteering are often called, "The Thinking Sport." In Brainerd Minnesota there is an orienteering area. Out in the woods, being able to run like a deer is not important. Making wise decisions is most important. You must rely on reading the map choosing routes, and recognizing the territory.

Editing Practice

Practice your editing skills below after completing the lesson on pages 5 – 8.

I Never Said I Wasn't Difficult

■ ■

Here are two paragraphs a student wrote about reading poetry. There are mistakes in each paragraph. Some sentences may have one or more mistakes. Other sentences may contain no mistakes at all. <u>There are no mistakes in spelling.</u>

Read the paragraphs to find the mistakes. Draw a line through each mistake in the paragraph. Then write the correction above it.

John was feeling confused and angry. His Mother told him to read a poem.

It was called, *I Never Said I Wasn't Difficult*. John read the poem. Again and again.

Afterward, he thought, "gee, this guy is a lot like me."

John read some poems from the book called *poems for kids*. He told his mom

that a poem is a mystery. It doesn't say everything. " Your right," she said. Poets turn

words around, letting us see them from a different angle." Do you agree.

Editing Practice

Practice your editing skills below after completing the lesson on pages 9 – 14.

The Path to Knighthood

■ ■

Here are two paragraphs a student wrote about the Middle Ages. There are mistakes in each paragraph. Some sentences may have one or more mistakes. Other sentences may contain no mistakes at all. <u>There are no mistakes in spelling.</u>

Read the paragraphs to find the mistakes. Draw a line through each mistake in the paragraph. Then write the correction above it.

Minstrels were the entertainers of the middle ages. These musicians and singers traveled from town too town throughout Europe. Mimes performed plays jugglers sometimes juggled daggers. Acrobats, tumblers, and jesters traveled with the minstrels. Castles provided the perfect place for the entertainers.

The minstrels were known as troubadours in france. They composed music and wrote poems. The troubadours sang songs. About the love between knights and ladies. They're poems told of the gallant deeds the knights performed. They sang of the beautiful ladies who inspired those deeds.

Editing Practice

Practice your editing skills below after completing the lesson on pages 15 – 20.

Keeping a Journal:
Interview with Jack Gantos

■■■■■■■■■■■■■■■■■■■■■■■■■■■■■■■■■■

Here are two paragraphs a student wrote about keeping a journal. There are mistakes in each paragraph. Some sentences may have one or more mistakes. Other sentences may contain no mistakes at all. <u>There are no mistakes in spelling.</u>

Read the paragraphs to find the mistakes. Draw a line through each mistake in the paragraph. Then write the correction above it.

A journal is your own space. How you use it depends on who you are?

Writers use journals to spark his creativity. Travelers write about the places they've

been. Because they want to remember them. Scientists record their discoveries in

their journals to keep track of them.

What if you don't want to write. You can slip movie or ball game tickets onto a

page. Later, it reminded you of a certain day. Perhaps you'd rather draw or doodle a

memory. You can also clip out a poem and paste it in the book. Keep your own

memories. In your own style.

Editing Practice

Practice your editing skills below after completing the lesson on pages 21 – 24.

The Cave

■■■■■■■■■■■■■■■■■■■■■■■■■■■■■■■■■■■■

Here are two paragraphs a student wrote about poetry. There are mistakes in each paragraph. Some sentences may have one or more mistakes. Other sentences may contain no mistakes at all. <u>There are no mistakes in spelling.</u>

Read the paragraphs to find the mistakes. Draw a line through each mistake in the paragraph. Then write the correction above it.

Ancient people did not have printing presses. If they had news to tell. They wrote a poem about the event. Long ago, icelandic poets wrote their history in poems they called Sagas.   Storytellers could remember them and recite them. Poetry is easier to remember than prose. The poet use rhyme and rhythm to make his work easy to remember.

Metaphors are images, the poet chooses images that stick in the mind. Metaphors makes a connection between two things that are not really alike. To remember something, you often connect it to something you knows and can remember easily.

Editing Practice

Practice your editing skills below after completing the lesson on pages 25 – 28.

The Earth Is Really Moving

■■■■■■■■■■■■■■■■■■■■■■■■■■■■■■■■■■■■

Here are two paragraphs a student wrote about science. There are mistakes in each paragraph. Some sentences may have one or more mistakes. Other sentences may contain no mistakes at all. <u>There are no mistakes in spelling.</u>

Read the paragraphs to find the mistakes. Draw a line through each mistake in the paragraph. Then write the correction above it.

A bike will not budge unless it is touched. After it starts, it will not stop.   What happens when you jump off a moving bike. It keeps moving in a straight line at a steady speed it continues on until it falls over. This proves sir Isaac Newton's first Law of Motion. Things in motion tend to stay in motion.

Isaac Newton was born in Lincolnshire England. He loved science and Mathematics. Newton had one of the most brilliant minds of all time. He discovered that gravity is a force. It keeps us tied to the Earth. And controls the motion of planets and stars.

Editing Practice

Practice your editing skills below after completing the lesson on pages 29 – 34.

It All Depends on How You Look At It

■ ■

Here are two paragraphs a student wrote about cartoons. There are mistakes in each paragraph. Some sentences may have one or more mistakes. Other sentences may contain no mistakes at all. <u>There are no mistakes in spelling.</u>

Read the paragraphs to find the mistakes. Draw a line through each mistake in the paragraph. Then write the correction above it.

Not all cartoons are meant to entertain. Political cartoons is sometimes very powerful. There purpose is to persuade. Benjamin Franklin drew America's first political cartoon, a snake cut in pieces. It said "Join or Die." Its purpose was to have the colonies join together in the french and indian war.

Doug Marlette is also a political cartoonist. Did you know that his cartoons appear in many newspapers. Marlette say he started cartooning as a child. By the time he is sixteen, he was learning from copying. The cartoonist calls his work a "visual rock 'n' roll."

Unit 5 Test
Reading
Listening
Writing
Editing

The test you are about to take is designed to examine your ability to read, listen, and write effectively. It is no different from the exercises you have done throughout this book. Use the note-taking and test-taking strategies you have learned to demonstrate your improved skills in all three areas!

Stay calm and focused.
You will do a great job!

```
******************************************
*                                        *
*          Test: Part I                  *
*          Reading                       *
*                                        *
******************************************
```

In this part of the test you are going to read an article about cooking with the sun, a poem, and a story about an outcast. Then you will answer some questions about what you have read.

*You may look back
at the selections
as often as you like!*

Cooking with the Sun

by Jennifer Davidson

■■■■■■■■■■■■■■■■■■■■■■■■■■■■■■■■■■■■■■

When Dr. Robert Metcalf first used a solar cooker, the future changed for thousands—maybe millions—of Africans.

He knew that billions of poor people around the world depend on the use of wood for cooking. And as they take more and more firewood from wild areas, they are destroying habitats around the world.

"Sunshine can be an alternative to fire," Dr. Metcalf says. He has helped people around the world to use simple new technologies to cook their food and make their water safe to drink—without burning wood.

Villagers Hard at Work

Each morning in villages across East Africa, small children and their mothers wake up and walk several miles to collect firewood to cook their food. Their journey takes much of the day, and the heavy bundles they carry home on their heads last only a few days.

This is why Dr. Metcalf spends each summer in Africa. He teaches women and children in villages and refugee camps how to cook with the sun.

He knows the importance of cooking to make food safe. He is a scientist who studies germs. He wanted to help answer two important questions: How can more people cook without fire? And how can they make sure their drinking water is safe?

He helped create Solar Cookers International. This organization introduces solar cookers to developing countries. It teaches people how to use them.

Technology That's Easy

In the district of Nyakach in Kenya, women use sunlight to cook their traditional meals of ground white corn, or *ugali*, which is mixed with rice, beans, and vegetables.

Instead of building a fire, they mix the food in a dark pot, put the pot into a clear plastic bag, and place the pot and bag in a solar cooker. The cooker is an open box, lined with aluminum foil and shaped to reflect sunlight onto the pot. The dark surface of the pot absorbs much of the light. This turns the light energy into heat, which cooks the food.

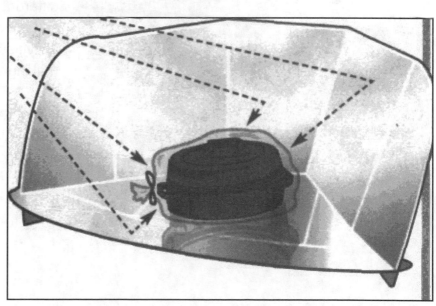

The solar cooker is made of cardboard and lined with aluminum foil. This reflects the sun's ray onto a dark pot in a clear plastic bag. The heat cooks the food.

"The women are very excited because it's easy, it works, and the food tastes great," says Dr. Metcalf. So far, more than thirty thousand African families now have solar cookers, and new programs will introduce solar cookers to millions of families.

Making Water Safe

To find water, women and children may have to walk long distances. They fill their buckets and carry them home on their heads. The buckets often weigh as much as forty pounds. Not only is finding water hard work, but the water is often contaminated with germs that make people sick.

Dr. Metcalf and others developed a simple, reusable device that people can use to make sure their water is safe to drink. The device is called a WAPI, which stands for "Water Pasteurization Indicator." It is used to be sure water is safe to drink.

In this process, harmful germs in water are killed by heating the water to 149 degrees Fahrenheit for one minute. That's not boiling, but it's too hot to touch.

But many people in Africa do not have thermometers. They can use a WAPI instead. It's a closed plastic tube with a ball of hard wax stuck inside one end. To pasteurize a pot of water, anyone can lower a WAPI into the pot and slowly  heat the water in a solar cooker. When the ball of wax melts and drops to the bottom of the tube, the water has reached a temperature that kills the bacteria. To use the WAPI again, the user turns it over so that the wax is in the upper end of the tube.

According to Dr. Metcalf, "The women in Nyakach say, 'The sun is shining in a different way in East Africa.' The relentless sun is now an ally in two of the most important activities humans share—cooking food and making water safe."

There is much more work to be done. But thanks to Dr. Metcalf and Solar Cookers International, the lives of many East Africans are becoming safer and easier, one village at a time.

Objective Questions

Circle the letter next to the correct answer.

1. This article is MAINLY about?
   a. helping an African village
   b. using a renewable source of energy
   c. saving endangered species
   d. Dr. Metcalf and Solar Cookers International

2. According to the article, solar cooking is highly valuable because:
   a. it does not work in the rain
   b. it is less work than burning wood
   c. it makes food taste better
   d. it destroys bacteria and saves the environment

3. The information in this article suggests that black pots are best because:
   a. they are inexpensive
   b. they trap the most heat
   c. they are heavier
   d. people prefer them

4. Based on this story, the reader can conclude that the Kenyan diet is largely:
   a. vegetarian
   b. dependent on meat
   c. uncooked
   d. unhealthy

5. What function does the wax have in the design of the WAPI?
   a. It acts as a lid.
   b. It traps the heat.
   c. It keeps track of temperature.
   d. It kills germs.

Continue...

6. Read the following sentence from the story.

   The relentless sun is now an ally in two of the most important activities humans share–cooking food and making water safe.

   The word "ally" means about the same as:
   a. part of
   b. friend
   c. necessary
   d. unhelpful

7. Why is Africa an ideal place for solar heaters?
   a. The availability of tropical sunlight
   b. The Solar Cookers International have centers there.
   c. The people are very willing to try new things.
   d. There are no rainforests left.

8. According to this article many African villagers will have safe food and water in the future.

   Which statement below best supports that conclusion?
   a. The lives of many East Africans are becoming safer and easier.
   b. They place the pot and bag in a solar cooker.
   c. Dr. Metcalf and others developed a simple, reusable device called a WAPI.
   d. There is much more work to be done.

9. Read the following sentence from the story:

   The women in Nyakach say, "The sun is shining in a different way in East Africa."

   What do they mean by the statement?
   a. The climate is changing.
   b. The sun has become a danger.
   c. New use of the sun is changing their lives.
   d. They have found ways to replace the sun.

10. How may the rest of the world benefit from Dr. Metcalf's work?
    a. The sun will shine brighter.
    b. Water may be more plentiful.
    c. New sources of food will be found.
    d. Fewer animals may become extinct.

Four Little Foxes

by Lew Sarett

This poem was written for a specific purpose. Can you tell its purpose?

Speak gently, Spring, and make no sudden sound;
For in my windy valley, yesterday I found
Newborn foxes squirming on the ground-
  Speak gently.

Walk softly, March, forbear the bitter blow;
Her feet within a trap, her blood upon the snow,
The four little foxes saw their mother go-
  Walk softly.

Go lightly, Spring, oh, give them no alarm;
When I covered them with boughs to shelter them from harm
The thin blue foxes suckled at my arm-
  Go lightly.

Step softly, March, with your rampant hurricane;
Nuzzling one another, and whimpering with pain,
The new little foxes are shivering in the rain-
  Step softly.

Objective Questions

Circle the letter next to the correct answer.

1. In this poem who is the poet addressing?
   a. nature
   b. hunters
   c. the little foxes
   d. the missing mother

2. What had happened BEFORE the poet came upon the scene?
   a. The mother fox deserted her babies.
   b. The mother fox went in search of food.
   c. A large animal killed the mother fox.
   d. The mother fox stepped into a trap.

3. Which words from the poem are meant to indicate that the foxes were hungry?
   a. squirming on the ground
   b. suckled at my arm
   c. whimpering with pain
   d. shivering in the rain

4. How did the poet try to protect the foxes?
   a. He hid them.
   b. He fed them.
   c. He eased their pain.
   d. He took them home.

5. The tone of this poem is:
   a. threatening
   b. pleading
   c. loving
   d. questioning

6. The poet uses personification with the words:
   a. Her feet within a trap
   b. Nuzzling one another
   c. Speak gently, Spring
   d. whimpering with pain

7. Read the following line from the poem.

Step softly, March, with your rampant hurricane

The poet is asking March to:
a. be less fierce than usual
b. start the summer season
c. walk away
d. feed the little foxes

8. This poem is a complaint against:
a. foxes
b. spring's cruel weather
c. animal traps
d. wildlife

9. The reader can conclude that the poet:
a. is a ranger
b. went in search of the foxes
c. lives close by
d. saw the scene on TV

10. The last line of each stanza is a poetic techique called:
a. rhyme
b. simile
c. metaphor
d. repetition

The Outcast

■ ■

Young Tom was a lonely boy who lived long ago. A gurgling river flowed through his small hamlet. Whenever the townspeople had a holiday, they would climb up the hill behind the town. There they set up picnic benches beside the lake. Some boys and girls liked to take rowboats and canoes for a peaceful ride.

> hamlet = a very small village

Poor Tom never went with them. It wasn't that he was ugly or mean. It was just that he had such a funny voice; it squealed like a whistle when he spoke. No one could ever understand him. Usually they became so irate, they pushed him away.

One day, an old sage, a wise man with a long beard, came to town. Everyone gathered around to listen to his wise sayings. Tom squiggled his way through the crowd. "Surely this wise man can help me," thought Tom.

When everyone had gone home, Tom wrote a note to the sage. "How can I get a powerful voice that people will listen to?" it read.

"You must tell people some sensational news, something they really want to hear," responded the wise man.

Tom ran about the hamlet the next day, trying to get people to listen. They just shoved him aside. "You are annoying. We cannot understand you," they said.

Later that day, the sage found Tom, sulking on his doorstep. This time the wise one said, "Before anyone will listen to you, *you* must learn to listen."

> sulk = to pout or mope

For weeks Tom wandered through the fields and forest. He listened and listened. Soon he was able to understand the warble of the birds, the whisper of the wind, and the gossip of the beetles.

Again, he aproached the town. Now he really had wonders to tell people. Alas, again he was disappointed. People just ignored him. They didn't even bother to shoo him away.

By this time the sage was on his way to another town. His farewell words to Tom were, "There is only one thing left for you to do. You must do something for people that they cannot do for themselves."

"Well, that will never happen," thought Tom. "I shall always be an outcast."

outcast = one who is tossed out by society

At that moment a crow whisked by. She darted back and forth, full of anxiety. "Flee for your lives!" she told the squirrels and the hares. "Run for the hills!" she screeched at the dogs and the sheep.

"Why, why?" cried the animals.

cascade = to rush down in a great quantity

"The rains have filled the lake above. The lake will cascade down into the river and over the banks. Run! Run!"

Only Tom understood. He put his ear to the ground and heard the rumble of the river. It was swelling and growing, crashing toward town. But who would listen to him?

With strength that only fear could give him, Tom began to heave great boulders and logs into the river. Suddenly, for a moment the town was silent. Then everyone grabbed rocks and branches, and soon a dam was built across the river. The town was saved from the flood.

Tom's voice was the same as it always had been. Yet, it was the clearest voice in the hamlet.

Objective Questions

Circle the letter next to the correct answer.

1. What made Tom an outcast?
   a. his annoying habits
   b. his appearance
   c. his speech
   d. his thoughts

2. When did Tom's troubles begin?
   a. when the sage came to town
   b. when he whispered
   c. when he understood the birds
   d. long before the sage came to town

3. Read the following sentence from the story.

   No one could ever understand him. Usually they became so irate, they pushed him away.

   The word "irate" means about the same as:
   a. disgusted
   b. angry
   c. saddened
   d. busy

4. The theme of this story is:
   a. Do not undervalue anyone.
   b. This is how to prevent disaster.
   c. It pays to listen to animals.
   d. Extraordinary strength comes in time of trouble.

5. What two things changed Tom's life?
   a. He spoke to the sage; he did not follow his advice.
   b. He asked for a big voice; the sage gave him one.
   c. He gave up on the villagers; he sulked on his doorstep.
   d. He learned to listen; he had important news to tell.

6. Read the following sentence from the story.

> **With strength that only fear could give him, Tom began to heave great boulders and logs into the river.**

This means that:
 a. Tom was afraid he could not persuade the others to help.
 b. Tom used the splashing logs to warn the town.
 c. Angry at the townspeople, Tom threw boulders into the river.
 d. Tom grew stronger because he was so afraid.

7. How did the townspeople change in this story?
 a. They became stronger.
 b. They learned about fear.
 c. They learned to listen.
 d. They never worked hard again.

8. Which struggle below describes the MAIN conflict in this story?
 a. Tom wants to be heard; no one will pay attention.
 b. The river is flooding; the town is not aware.
 c. The sage gives advice; Tom can't make it work.
 d. The townspeople need help; Tom provides the support.

9. The main conflict is resolved when:
 a. Tom learns to listen to the animals around him.
 b. Tom decides it is better to be an outcast.
 c. Tom does something for the villagers they cannot do for themselves.
 d. Tom asks the sage for help with his problems.

10. When Tom "squeals" again, the people will most likely:
 a. become annoyed with him
 b. listen carefully to what he says
 c. ignore his message
 d. check the river again

```
************************************************
*                                              *
*            Test: Part II                     *
*            Listening                         *
*                                              *
*                                              *
************************************************
```

In this part of the test your teacher will read a story two times. Listen carefully. Then you will answer some questions about the story.

As you listen, it helps
to picture the story
in your mind.

Listening Comprehension
A Greek Myth: The Trojan Horse

Listening Directions

You are going to listen to a story called, "The Trojan Horse." The story will be read twice. You may take notes on the story anytime during the two readings. You may use your notes to answer the questions that follow.

Characters in the story:
Helen = wife of the King of Greece and the most beautiful woman in the world
Athena = a Greek goddess

Notes

Notes

■ ■

Short Response Questions

Use the information from the story to answer the questions below.

1. Fill in the details of the chart below to show the cause and effect of the abduction of Helen.

CAUSE	EFFECT

2. Today, the Trojan horse has become a symbol of trickery. Explain why this is so.

_____

_____

_____

_____

_____

_____

_____

Short Response Questions

■■■■■■■■■■■■■■■■■■■■■■■■■■■■■■■

3. Did this myth convince you that there really was a Trojan horse? Explain why or why not.

_____

_____

_____

_____

_____

_____

_____

Essay

■ ■

In this story, a famous Trojan prophet said, "Never trust a Greek bearing gifts."
Did his warning prove to be true or false? Explain why.

In your essay, be sure to include the following:
- Discuss the events that led to this statement.
- Did the events that followed prove him right or wrong?
- Explain why.

Use information from the story to support your answer.

_____

_____

_____

_____

_____

_____

_____

_____

_____

_____

_____

GO ON to page 122 if you need more space.

Essay

■■■■■■■■■■■■■■■■■■■■■■■■■■■■■■■■■■■■

_____

_____

_____

_____

_____

_____

_____

_____

_____

_____

_____

_____

_____

_____

_____

_____

```
*************************************************

         Test: Part III
           Writing

*************************************************
```

In this part of the test you will read an article and a poem about whales. You will answer some questions about what you have read. Then you will write an essay using information from both selections.

> *You may look back at the article and poem as often as you like.*

Whale Watching in Hawaii

It's winter and we're on a whale watch aboard *Swaying Sails*, off the coast of Maui in Hawaii. It is a pink dawn as we board our sailboat and Lisa, our guide, points to a tall spout of water off on the horizon. This is the first sign that there are whales in the area. The humpback whale is letting air out of its two-part blowhole. Because a whale is a mammal, it has to breathe air. When it touches the surface of the ocean, it breathes out air, making a blow, or a spout. It draws huge lungfuls of air through the blowholes, then closes them tightly and is ready to submerge, or go under again.

Humpbacks live in all oceans of the world. But the ones we're hoping to spy are the western North American humpbacks.

A whale's spout can be seen from a distance.

We're pretty far out to sea now, although we can still see the people on the shore. All of a sudden, one of the whale watchers points screeching, "Look, look!"

We look just in time to see the humpback breach. This whale is very strong and lifts its body completely out of the water. All 53 tons crash back into the water as its body bends. That's how it gets its name, the hump-back. Some of those on board almost miss it and only look in time to see the flukes, the two halves of the tale fin. Each humpback has a different pattern on the bottom of its flukes.

The breaching humpback lifts its body out of the water.

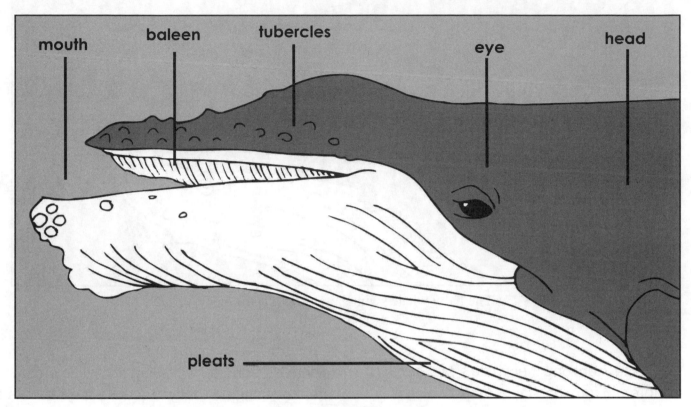

The Head of the Humpback

Now everyone is keeping his or her eyes peeled, hoping for more whales to perform. Meanwhile Lisa is sharing many interesting facts about this huge animal. She reports that if we could get close enough, we would see that they have small eyes located just about at the corner of their mouths.

We would notice that their throats have about 25 *pleats,* or grooves, that get larger to allow the whale to ingest hundreds of pounds of krill in one giant swallow.

Krill, tiny shrimp-like fish, is a favorite meal for the humpback. Because it is daylight for 24 hours every day during the summer up in the polar regions, tiny sea plants grow in abundance, or large numbers. Krill and other small shell fish feed on them.

The krill travel in huge schools. When the whale catches up with them, his mouth can hold hundreds of pounds of krill. This type of whale has no teeth. He has *baleen,* two rows of flat bony plates with hairlike fringes that hang down from the top of the mouth. The baleen screens out the krill which slide down the gullet. The water is spit out.

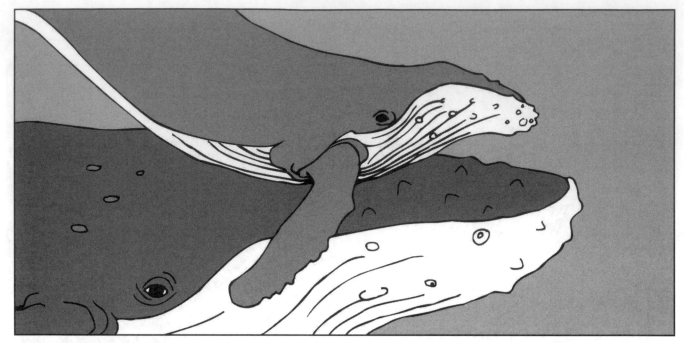

The baby whale swims just above its mother.

Lisa mentions the whale's *blubber*, a thick three to four inch layer of fat, which is accumulated during the summer. This stored fat is what the whale lives on during the entire winter. When darkness comes to the North, the food supply dwindles, and the western humpback whale heads south for the warm Pacific waters. Here, it eats very little.

This is when the whales mate. The male sings a song which can be heard for many miles. The melody is complicated, with many high and low notes. When two humpbacks find the right mate, they reach out their long flippers, which can be 15 feet long, and touch each other. They splash together in the water just as though they were dancing.

Baby whales, or *calves* are born here. The baby humpback knows how to swim the minute it's born. It swims just above its mother, often touching her body. Because the whale is a mammal, she nurses her baby.

Lisa reports that it's a little lonely on Maui when winter is over and the cycle repeats itself. The whales head north for the summer. Often a male accompanies the mother and calf and stays with them for the summer. He's called an escort.

Humpback whales have been known to make these trips for more than 30 years. The big bumps on old whales' bodies are *barnacles,* small sea animals with shells, which like to attach themselves to humpback whales. They do not harm the whale; they just hang on, catching their food from the surrounding water.

We were lucky to to be sailing right in season.

Short Response Questions

Use the information from the story to answer the questions below.

1. Give two reasons migrating south is important for the whale? Why does it swim back to the North every year?

_____

_____

_____

_____

_____

2. Why is whale watching so fascinating to many people? What do they expect too see?

_____

_____

_____

_____

_____

Sea Canary

by Jane Yolen

■■■■■■■■■■■■■■■■■■■■■■■■■■■■■■■■■■■■■

The white whale, or beluga, was called the sea canary by eighteenth-century English whalers for its chirps, whistles, and moans could be heard above the water. For hundreds of years it has been hunted for its meat. It is almost extinct.

We heard her, white and weary,

singing a last song,

her whistle following us

into the night.

Did she sing of her young

still brown behind her?

Or of the bottoms of waves

made light by the moon?

Or did she sing her death,

the harps still heavy in her bones,

pulling her towards the air

and the long dark shanks of our hold.

Short Answer Questions

■ ■

Use the information from the poem to answer the questions below.

3. Fill in the chart below to explain the sea canary problems.

Sea canary's problem	
How it communicates its distress	
The speaker's emotions	

Prewriting Notes

■ ■

You may use this space to organize your thoughts for the essay on the next page.

Combined Essay

■ ■

After reading the article "Whale Watching in Hawaii" and the poem, "Sea Canary," the reader may want to protect the whale. Write an essay in which you try to convince others to protect the whale.

In your essay, be sure to include:
- a description of the whale
- why there is a need to protect whales
- how you would accomplish this

Be sure to use information in BOTH the story and the poem to support your answer.

_____

_____

_____

_____

_____

_____

_____

_____

_____

_____

_____

Essay

Test: Part IV
Editing

Here are two paragraphs a student wrote . There are mistakes in each paragraph. Some sentences may have one or more mistakes. Other sentences may contain no mistakes at all. <u>There are no mistakes in spelling.</u>

Read the paragraphs to find the mistakes. Draw a line through each mistake in the paragraph. Then write the correction above it.

There are many different sign languages in the world. Each country have

its own. On May 17 2006, my friend left for a trip around the world. She is hearing

impaired, she uses American Sign Language. Unfortunately, she will not understand

Spanish Sign Language.

The Tucson Wildlife Center helps wildlife. That are injured sick, or orphaned.

The Center specializes in capturing and treating dangerous animals like eagles and

mountian lions. Director Smith of the Center says, "Our staff of volunteer veterinarians

nurse the animals back to health.

Editor's Page

Congratulations! You have written a wonderful first draft. Now it's time to polish your writing. Follow the checklist below, to add the finishing touch.

Read your story aloud and circle your answer.

Y   N   **Did you stick to the topic?**
(Does every sentence belong?)
(Cut out any stray sentences!)

Y   N   **Can you think of a better way to say some things?**
(Just cross them out. Change and add details!)

Y   N   **Is the sentence a good one?**
(Correct it in the margins.)

Y   N   **Can you add descriptive adjectives and adverbs?**
(Underline a few plain nouns and verbs. Then go back
and think of some exciting adjectives and adverbs for them.
Use the ^ sign to show where they go!)

Y   N   **Did you use the same word over and over?**
(Do three sentences in a row start the same?)
(If you can't think of a synonym, try a thesaurus!)

*Remember, your first try is
never your best.
Bet it sounds
much better now!*